Tom and Ly[Wilson

Negotiate Anything!

Secrets to make businesses

treat you fairly

and for businesses ...

how to pull ahead of the competition

through excellent customer service

**SAXONY-
COBURN**
Since 1987

"NEGOTIATE ANYTHING!"

Published in the U.S. by Saxony-Coburn

PRINTED IN THE UNITED STATES OF AMERICA

First edition published 2010

ISBN 978-0-9846185-0-7

LCCN 2010911360

SAN 859-9394

SAXONY-
COBURN

333 North Commercial Street
Suite 350
Neenah, WI 54956
1-800-985-1353

www.caregiverpartnership.com/negotiate-anything.aspx

tomw@caregiverpartnership.com

lynnw@caregiverpartnership.com

This book is dedicated to every consumer who puts his trust in an organization — profit, nonprofit or medical — by laying down his hard-earned money with the expectation of good service, honesty and getting that money's worth.

We would like to thank Jennifer Knaack for her excellent copy editing skills, attention to detail and thoughts on many of the creative aspects of this book.

We would also like to thank Shiloh Schoon for his imaginative and creative illustrations, which helped bring the examples to life while providing a bit of tongue-in-cheek humor that most of us can relate to.

Praise for "Negotiate Anything!"

"'Negotiate Anything!' reminds everyone of how it used to be and how it should be now. This book is filled with practical examples and anecdotes that illuminate how well and how poorly many companies treat their customers. It also lets you know the tricks some companies use to bamboozle you and keep you from getting the good service you deserve. Through the example of The CareGiver Partnership, we learn how a company that cares about its customers is winning with impeccable, personalized service. A must-read for consumers, and more importantly, for customer service managers and executives!"

Jim Ebel
Chief Marketing Officer, University of Mississippi
Founder of CenterBrain Partners, Inc. and author of
"CenterBrain Thinking"

"As consumers become more conscious of their spending habits and look for increasing value for their money, they are demanding a higher quality level of service from the companies they purchase products from. 'Negotiate Anything!' is a well-timed book that provides consumers with clear, actionable steps to ensure they receive the level of service they deserve. It is unique in that it also challenges business owners to rethink the cost-savings strategies that have been driven by technology over the past two decades, and to instead focus on the increased profitability that comes from creating strong, loyal customers through 'old-fashioned' customer service."

Steve Carlson
Former Senior Vice President, Marketing, HSBC
Principal, Sung Carlson Associates: A management
consulting firm specializing in increasing customer value

"Finally … a common-sense approach to what should be innately simple, yet American companies are spending millions of dollars every year trying to figure it out! 'Negotiate Anything!' empowers the consumer with practical recommendations to resolve problems and ultimately get what they deserve. Better yet … a read that could serve as a textbook to customer experience executives, helping their companies avoid the pitfalls of poor customer service. Let the seller beware."

> **Richard Worick**
> President/CEO, The MSR Group, a national market
> research firm specializing in the measurement and
> improvement of customer satisfaction and advocacy

"Tom and Lynn's perspective and insights will help every business leader realize the impact customer service has on a brand. It can fuel significant revenue growth. As an organization that handles over 15 million customer calls and 24 million e-mails, we will use the book to continue improving our customer relationships."

> **James F. Bere, Jr.**
> Chairman and CEO, Alta Resources, an international
> organization helping companies with customer support and
> more

Table of Contents

Foreword

THERE **are** **thousands** of books about customer service on Amazon.com, so when I was asked to write the foreword for "Negotiate Anything!" I was curious why the world needed yet another. But after reading just the first two chapters, I realized that "Negotiate Anything!" takes a very different approach in that it is two books in one — one for consumers and one for business leaders.

I have had over 20 years of experience leading a consumer services team for Kimberly-Clark Corporation. For many of those years, I worked with Tom Wilson while he was president of two of its global business sectors. As changes in modes of communication and product lines changed, our team included over 70 people at times. We handled 400,000 to 600,000 consumer contacts each year on brands including Kleenex, Huggies, Kotex, Depend and Poise products. I also met with Lynn and Tom shortly after they formed The CareGiver Partnership and was impressed with the type of service they were offering their customers — from answering all calls by the third ring, to using the customer's name and responding quickly to requests. Providing superior customer service is critical to the success of any organization.

"Negotiate Anything!" provides **consumers** with a simple process to get what they deserve when something goes wrong with a company, product or service. It also provides pragmatic steps that **businesses** of any size can implement to significantly enhance their customer service and use it as a sustainable competitive advantage. The authors point out the causes of deteriorating customer service and what consumers and business leaders can do to improve it.

By following the process presented in "Negotiate Anything!" consumers can see immediate benefits. The authors show how they, as consumers, have saved more than $30,000 using their simple process. The authors are so confident the process will work for anyone, they offer a money-back guarantee.

Many quantitative studies have proven that organizations with the best customer service have better business results — in gaining new customers via word of mouth, better retention, and higher sales growth rates and profit margins. The authors present a pragmatic process for continually enhancing customer service throughout the entire organization and using it as a differentiating competitive advantage.

"Negotiate Anything!" really nails what it takes to get a company to respond in a timely and appropriate fashion. In my role as director of consumer services at Kimberly-Clark, we appreciated it when a dissatisfied customer provided us with clear, well-articulated information about an issue she had with one of our products. At times, we responded to over 50,000 contacts in one month alone, so it is absolutely essential for consumer service team members to have accurate and complete information to provide a speedy response. While companies may have guidelines for compensating consumers for issues with their product or service, it can be helpful for consumers to be specific about what they expect as compensation. If a consumer is vague about his experience and what he wants, a company has to use its best judgment to provide compensation that may or may not meet a customer's expectations.

"Negotiate Anything!" points out how technology and cost-savings measures — such as the Internet, complicated phone systems, ticket kiosks and outsourcing — when misused actually deteriorate the delivery of customer service. Technology should enhance, not replace, the human factor, in many cases. Unfortunately, some organizations view customer service as an expense rather than a profit center. Therefore, anything that can be done to reduce expense is considered. Lower-cost service may include automated phone systems, expecting consumers to use FAQs to answer their own questions, making it difficult to locate a phone number to call the company, extending hold times and more.

For business leaders and owners, the authors present 12 success criteria that will make customer service a business driver rather than a cost center. The investment in customer service is no different than an investment in marketing, except it will likely have a greater and more sustainable result. A dollar invested toward a marketing tactic, such as a short-term price discount, can be easily and quickly copied by competitors, but the investment in an effective customer service approach may not be as easily replicated. The success criteria presented in this book include establishing customer service as a core business driver, ensuring that senior management leads and supports it, results are measured and reported, and employees are recognized when appropriate.

"Negotiate Anything!" is unique because of its duality of benefits to both consumers and business leaders. It will provide immediate financial benefits to consumers, which the authors guarantee in writing. Businesses, small and large, will realize sustainable volume and profit growth by implementing the 12 success criteria.

Cindy Van Grinsven
Former Director of Consumer Services
Kimberly-Clark Corporation

Secrets to make companies
treat you fairly.

Pull ahead of the competition through
excellent customer service.

Preface

WE **have been asked** many times, "Why did you write this book?" It was simple. In our personal lives, we've noticed a sharp deterioration of customer service. In the book, we explain why this has occurred. Tom is also a partner in one of the recognized best marketing consultancies: CenterBrain Partners, Inc., a 20-year-old practice that focuses on working with companies to help them position their products or services in the marketplace. CenterBrain has interviewed tens of thousands of consumers in markets across the United States over this period, in one-on-one discussions and quantitative surveys. It has clearly seen how frustrated consumers have become because of poor customer service. From the 1976 movie "Network," consumers are "mad as hell and they aren't going to take it anymore."

It would have been logical for a book about customer service to reflect a negative tone. We wanted the opposite — a positive message. A message that focuses on the solution, not the problem.

This book has two audiences. The first is for people like you and like us, everyday consumers who buy products and services as a matter of course in our daily lives and whose expectations are simply to receive what we were led to believe we should expect. We will share with you how to make your money work a lot harder by following simple steps to ensure that companies you do business with give you what they say they will.

This isn't a book about developing negotiating skills, although you will learn some tips. It isn't about becoming someone who rants, yells and complains — someone nobody wants to do business with. It's about getting what you are promised, in an unemotional, process-oriented, fact-based manner.

You will learn the process, strategies, and steps we have developed and refined over the past 30 years. Throughout the book, we've included a number of actual examples we've had with all types of businesses. We've included some of the correspondence, such as letters and e-mails we've written, as well as some of the responses we've received. We did this because it is important to see firsthand the amount of follow-up and obsessive brute persistence that is required to *Get Your Money's Worth*. Our correspondence provides a template for the type of information and the tone and manner in which you need to communicate in order to balance future outcomes in your favor.

The other audience for this book is business owners — from small shop owners to CEOs of Fortune 500 companies and their deputies. This book will provide you with an idea of what your organization may be putting us consumers though. For you, we've developed a simple process that, if implemented, will give you an important and differential advantage vs. your competition. For some reason, organizations turn over every stone looking for a competitive edge, but most don't consider, really consider, customer service as an option. Service is how IBM originally became successful.

In 2004, we identified a need to help caregivers and their loved ones provide home care. There was a large unmet need for access to resources, experts, and a place to find answers to caregiver questions relating to products and supplies used in a home care setting. We spent two years talking with caregivers throughout the United States about how we could best meet their needs, then formed The CareGiver Partnership, a national direct-to-consumer retailer of a broad range of products, services and resources.

We built The CareGiver Partnership with a singular focus on providing a whole new level of service to caregivers and their loved ones — what we coined as Personalized Attention℠ service — 1950s style. Research we conducted with caregivers (consumers) in cities across the United States clearly showed the majority were women, and they were

14   "A complaint is a gift."

upset about customer service calls being outsourced to countries where they couldn't understand the person on the other end of the phone, then talking to someone who wasn't knowledgeable. It annoyed them to push buttons, make choices, then wait on hold, listening to prerecorded messages about how important they are to a company. Caregivers are frustrated, frantic and frazzled.

With these insights in mind, we designed our service to make their lives a bit easier. We hired only women who had been, or were currently, caregivers to a family member or loved one. These are our Product Specialists, who work in our Wisconsin-based in-house call center. Our customers appreciate that our specialists speak clearly and slowly for those hard of hearing. Imagine an 80-year-old who is hard of hearing talking to someone in a foreign country who speaks in a low tone with a thick accent.

Most importantly, our caregivers want to speak to someone who is knowledgeable. That's why each of our Product Specialists receives ongoing training on every product we offer. Training occurs via in-services from manufacturers' reps who visit our training center, online and printed training aids, and teleconferences with manufacturers. Our team is given samples of many of the products so, when talking with a customer, they can speak from experience rather than relying on scripts, of which we have none.

We made a strategic decision to dismantle all the fancy features of our state-of-the-art phone system and simply answer all calls by the third ring — but usually the first or second. While making a presentation to an executive MBA class, a student said he ran a phone center for his company and that our operation could be more efficient if we forced people to wait on hold while our Product Specialists were busy with other customers. Our response was that our service is a key differentiator, and we are willing to invest in having sufficient staff available to answer customers' calls right away.

We also use a returning customer's first name in many cases when they call us. While on the phone with a customer, we write all orders on paper, rather typing them into the computer. This allows our Product Specialists to have a personalized and interactive discussion, and avoids the distracting background noise of a keyboard clicking and clacking. Our Product Specialists also sit in high-profile work spaces that are about three to four times larger than most call-center stations, to eliminate most distracting background noise, such as other conversations and ringing phones.

This book is not about The CareGiver Partnership, but you will learn how we have incorporated much of the learning from our personal customer service experience into crafting the company. We like to think that we at The CareGiver Partnership are so passionate about customer service, we literally wrote the book on it. With this in mind ...

Most consumers' expectations are simple. For example, when a service organization says the repairperson will be at your home "in the morning," to the average person this means before noon. How many times have you been frustrated that they can't be more precise, such as say between 10 and 11 a.m.? This holds true for medical professionals as well.

Have you then waited around until 1 p.m. or so, then finally called, only to have a rude person tell you they must be running behind and should be there shortly? You wonder, with the number of cell phones in the United States today, doesn't this repairperson have one? Or why doesn't someone at the office call? Why? Because you are not that important to them.

The title of one of Bill O'Reilly's books, "Who's Looking Out For You?" is a good question to ask. It has to be you, because they aren't. There was an example in the fall of 2007 where a woman could not get the "fantastic" service promised by her high-speed Internet and phone provider. When she went to the provider's office to discuss, she was told to sit and wait for a manger to meet with her. A while later she was told he'd gone home. She came back the next day with a hammer. Needless to say, this isn't a strategy we recommend, but it does illustrate how awful service has become and its effect on customers.

This book was a passion of ours, not intended to be a moneymaker. No one in their right minds would want to spend 30 years gathering information, not to mention the time spent organizing and writing the book. Especially when there are thousands of books for sale on Amazon.com with the phrase "customer service" in the title. Here is a list of some of the biggest sellers and why this book is unique:

"Customer Experience Management: A Revolutionary Approach to Connecting With Your Customers"

"Customer Satisfaction Is Worthless, Customer Loyalty Is Priceless: How to Make Customers Love You, Keep Them Coming Back and Tell Everyone They Know"

"Call Center Success: Essential Skills for CSRs"

"The Big Book of Customer Service Training Games: Quick, Fun Activities for Training Customer Service Reps, Salespeople, and Anyone Else Who Deals With Customers"

As you can see from the titles above, most books about customer service are written as a how-to guide for businesses. What sets "Negotiate Anything!" apart is that it is that it is written for two audiences: consumers *and* business leaders. It is written to these two audiences in the hopes of improving the customer service process from end to end — from the interaction between the consumer and the company, during the shopping and purchase process, then between the company and consumer if an issue arises. Consumers will be delighted, and businesses that begin to leverage customer service as a differentiator will thrive. Business leaders need to know what's wrong and how to fix it. On the other hand, consumers need to apply pressure to help provide the incentive for businesses to improve their service. Otherwise it's business as usual. You need to expect and demand more.

For consumers, we've provided time-tested strategies on how to interact with companies to significantly improve getting your money's worth in the process.

For business leaders, we explain why customer service has seriously eroded and its causes. Then we present strategies to significantly improve sustainable business growth by transforming organizations toward becoming the best in the world at providing customer service within their industries.

"No, that's not right ... you're supposed to put tab A into slot D ... I think, but I don't see a slot D. How in the heck are our customers supposed to put this thing together?"

Chapter 1
Why a Primer on Customer Service?

WE **didn't wake** up one day and decide to write this book. The genesis occurred in 1978, while Tom was working in marketing for Colgate-Palmolive and was privy to consumer complaints and insights about such brands as Dynamo detergent, Colgate toothpaste and Palmolive dishwashing liquid. Lynn had worked in customer service in the banking industry. While at Colgate, Tom was fortunate to be able to go to shopping malls in the New York City area every few months and spend a day with consumers, talking about the brand he was working on at the time, during which he would get an earful. Consumers tell it like it is, and those who use a particular brand frequently know more about it than many of the people who work at the company.

That's when it dawned on us: The person responsible for all aspects of a brand, the product manager, needed to be intimately familiar with all aspects of it. This included using it frequently, buying it, reading the packaging for clarity, opening the packaging to see how it functions and discarding it. In other words, they need to "be one" with the brand. This same concept applies to any business, whether manufacturing, service or intangibles like insurance and banking products. A company and its employees should be intimate with all aspects of their brand. And those of its competitors.

Eventually Tom took a job at Kimberly-Clark Corporation and was responsible for several big brands, including Huggies diapers and baby wipes, Kotex feminine care, and Depend and Poise incontinence products. Lynn worked on the front lines at Dayton's, Marshall Field & Co., and Macy's for 11 years. Some of the most passionate consumers of Kimberly-Clark brands were the ones who wrote about their experiences with the Depend and Poise brands. Tom enjoyed taking the time to write and phone them to learn what issues they had with the products and marketing policies.

While he was at Kimberly-Clark, the company would receive between 40,000 and 60,000 consumer contacts each month, all answered by friendly "Cheeseheads" in Neenah, Wisconsin.

Tom made it a practice to meet with those who were on the front line, talking with consumers every day. He made it a point to regularly listen to consumer calls, gaining keen insights into the company's brands and what needed to be changed with the product design, description, packaging and marketing. As an officer of Kimberly-Clark, he felt this was one of his most important accountabilities. He was disappointed that many of those in management didn't take the time to listen to consumers or find it all that important.

During the very early days of the Internet, Tom led the team that built Kimberly-Clark's first corporate Web site. He insisted from day one that Kimberly-Clark provide consumers with an opportunity to contact the company online with complaints and product suggestions. This doesn't seem remarkable today, but was novel at the time. He also insisted the company provide an immediate confirmatory response, with the final resolution occurring within 24 hours.

Tom and the team who responded to consumers were all surprised how quickly the Internet contact grew. The director of consumer services asked Tom to forecast the number of Internet contacts her team should expect on a monthly basis. He had benchmarked numbers from another consumer products company and told her to plan on 100. It quickly exceeded 1,000. Why did this happen? It was simply a more convenient way for consumers to communicate with the company. Kimberly-Clark still provided toll-free access and, of course, snail mail.

Unfortunately, some companies don't set high standards for customer service. In early 2004, we wrote to a major airline based in the United States, one of the world's largest airlines in fact, about a travel issue. The company promptly sent a letter confirming they had received ours. Good start, but regrettably, it didn't follow up with a final response until 63 days after our initial contact — clearly not placing a great deal of emphasis on customer service.

Back to how we got started with this, the late 1970s. We started paying close attention to how companies and their employees delivered against customer service. Experiences ranged from downright deceit to mostly poor execution, driven by insufficient numbers of customer service employees that were poorly trained and not empowered to make decisions. They also were provided with an incomplete tool set and ineffective operational systems to assist them.

At some point along the way, we thought someday we would write a book about this. We began by maintaining a file of correspondence and keeping detailed notes about customer service issues we encountered, finally making time to assemble this early in the morning and during any free time we could find.

Because we've been collecting examples of good and bad customer service for 30 years, they span all types of businesses and service organizations, both for-profit and nonprofit. Our observation is that customer service, as an organizational process isn't getting better; it's getting worse. And technology has eroded, not enhanced, it.

The common denominator required to deliver outstanding customer service is having a sufficient number of intelligent, highly trained and empowered employees at the front end. Organizations are moving in the opposite direction. The Internet age, which stormed in during the 1990s, changed the way many companies do business. The buzzwords today are standardize, simplify, streamline. Others include outsource, cost-manage, efficiency, automate, downsize and right size. You don't hear a great deal about being the best at providing customer service. A U.S. airline announced in June 2004 that it was replacing 200 gate agents with machines. Nice efficiency, we're sure. Goodbye, customer service. God forbid you need to ask someone a question. We can hear them pleading, "But we need to cut costs to stay in business." Keep cutting costs and you may be out of business.

Midwest Express was a premier airline in the United States for years, consistently rated No. 1 by fliers. It also ranked No. 2 or 3 in the world. Its unique selling proposition, and advertising tag line, was "Best Care in the Air." During the 2008 recession, its CEO began changing aspects of the service that were the airline's differentiator, making the seats narrower and reducing leg room and cutting out meals, free newspapers, and complimentary wine and champagne. Over a five-year period, Midwest Express became "Parity Care in the Air," trying to compete on price, which they couldn't. In April 2010, owner Republic Airways discontinued the brand and grounded the Midwest fleet due to inefficiencies. Midwest management had made the same mistake Kmart did when it tried to compete against Wal-Mart on price — it couldn't. Meanwhile, retailers such as Target continued to focus on differentiation and customer service, and built strong brand equity.

Today, you are forced to pass through a gauntlet of online and telephone options before you can actually speak with a person. Companies expect you to review their Web sites' frequently asked questions, or call an automated phone system with level upon level of numbers to key in to locate the right person or department.

Once we called an information technology corporation and the recording told us it was experiencing unusually high call volume and our wait would be at least five minutes. That's kind of like hearing a partial score for a football game. Green Bay, 14 ... doesn't tell you very much. We'd prefer knowing how long a wait will be. For example, "Your hold time will be between five and eight minutes." They've got plenty of statisticians who develop complex algorithms; we're sure they can figure this one out. By the way, have you ever heard a recording say, "Good news! Our call volume is really low today and we'll be right with you"? That's why at The CareGiver Partnership we answer virtually all calls by the third ring.

The reason you're forced to wait on hold is due to poor planning and the fact that they've determined, based on quantitative market research studies, that you'll wait a certain number of minutes before hanging up. To maximize efficiencies, they plan their resources to manage to this level.

In this book, we use the word "governor" several times. We define it as a device that can be installed on vehicles to maintain the speed of an engine or to keep it from going above a specific level by controlling the fuel or steam supply. To govern is to control something by restraint. We use this term in this book to refer to the process that companies use to govern how they manage peaks and valleys of call demand. Rather than add more customer service representatives, many organizations govern the volume by increasing your hold time to specified targeted levels they feel you will put up with. Worse yet, some simply have recordings saying, "Our call volume is unusually high. Please call back later." Click. Nice personalized touch. Occasionally, calls at The CareGiver Partnership go to recording, but we don't keep people waiting on hold; we call them back, usually within 15 minutes.

Again, consumers become the governor for poor planning on the part of companies' customer service functions. Rather than have customer service representatives idle from time to time, companies force *us* to become their governor and sit and idle.

The last thing many companies want you to do today is to actually talk to someone. As the saying goes, time is money. To add insult to injury, some organizations have people in other countries providing customer service. Remember what we said about being intimate with your brand and what it takes to successfully deliver excellent customer service: intelligent, highly trained and empowered employees.

Outsourcing customer service saves money; that has been proven. In the long run, however, a company may have fewer customers calling, as they quit purchasing the brand due to poor customer service. Once an organization lets the "bean counters" take control of the business, they'll cost-save it to death. They get paid to reduce costs. Most bean counters couldn't tell you what brand equity is or why it's important. Because it is challenging to quantitatively measure, to them it isn't important. They can easily measure how much a call costs to answer in Bangalore, India, vs. Neenah, Wisconsin, however. Believe it or not, Neenah (pronounced *Nina*) is one of the leading call-center areas in the United States.

An example that comes to mind came from a friend who is a member of the American Automobile Association. He had a flat tire and called AAA to have someone come fix it. When he called to explain his location, it was evident he was talking to someone in a foreign country who couldn't find his location on a map. So much for the *American* Automobile Association. The least the organization could have done was provide proper training and require an adequate level of communication skills.

Through the CenterBrain Partners consulting practice, consumers of all types consistently tell us how much they dislike having their calls answered outside the United States. Outsourcing has its place and its limits.

Amazon.com is an example illustrating the lengths companies will go to in order to avoid having you actually talk with a person. We love Amazon and always have. We've purchased more merchandise than we planned on because they made it easy and fun. That was, until we needed to return something and went online to find out how. The options listed on its Web site didn't pertain to our situation, so we looked for a number to call. That turned into a "Where's Waldo?" situation. We searched all over the site and couldn't come up with a number. We then searched the Internet and found the number from someone else, who, as frustrated as we were, dug and dug until he found it. As a bonus for buying this book, the number is 800-201-7575.

Contrast the number of transactions being conducted in person in the 1950s with today. The Internet age, with exponentially increasing levels of online shopping, has virtually eliminated human contact as part of the transaction process. The airlines certainly don't want you to call; they have set the cost penalty so high that no one wants to purchase a ticket over the phone or at the counter. The little human contact that does occur is either via phone or online chat. As a result, there are fewer highly trained individuals who know how to provide excellent customer service. The art of personalized customer service has significantly declined since about 1990, especially in the digital age and after the birth of the Internet.

Think about times where you have been in a store and upon checking out you say thanks to the store associate. Frequently the only response you'll hear is "yup" or "no problem," or nothing at all. Do you ever ask yourself why you're thanking them and not the other way around? This amazes us; you step up to the counter and they say nothing. Why is that? It's simple: Companies don't recruit and train the right people or set high standards.

After staying at a few of the Four Seasons Hotels and Resorts, we realized if we asked an associate for something, he would respond with, "Certainly, it would be my pleasure." Wow. Six simple words that deliver so much. Sure beats "yup" or "no problem."

At The CareGiver Partnership, our vision to provide the best customer service includes making a return or problem-solving process as simple as an initial purchase. There are a number of companies that do this well, including L.L.Bean and Lands' End. We're sure there are many others, and if you believe you are one of them, please let us know.

How to get your _money's worth_

- ✓ Keep receipts
- ✓ Keep cartons, manuals
- ✓ Register new products
- ✓ Write to the CEO with issues
- ✓ Keep records of contacts
- ✓ Don't bid against yourself
- ✓ Ask for something specific
- ✓ Negotiate in baby steps
- ✓ Escalate if necessary

Chapter 2

Help Me. Please!

"You can't always get what you want,
But if you try sometime,
You just might find you get what you need."

— The Rolling Stones

WHEN you make a transaction, you have certain expectations. Most of the time these expectations are met. Unfortunately, many company policies are designed to work in favor of the company. While many companies talk about customer service — the customer is king, the customer is No. 1 — few have the policies, procedures, personnel, systems or tools in place to deliver against that promise. The only person looking out for your best interest is you. This book will help you resolve issues when they occur, and balance the outcome more in your favor than what you may be accustomed to. Accomplishing this requires time, patience and a process. Getting angry, causing a scene, name calling and talking in generalities are of little to no value to you.

If you follow the simple steps in this book, you will get more for your money in the long run. We guarantee it. You will also be part of a small army of consumers working to make companies more responsive and accountable to their shareholders, but also to their customers, who provide the healthy salaries, bonuses and stock options to the executives.

How to Get Your Money's Worth When Things Go Wrong

- Keep receipts at least for the length of the product's warranty.

- Keep original packaging, cartons and instruction manuals for a reasonable period of time, until you're sure a product meets your needs. If you want to return it, you'll need these items.

"A sale is not something you pursue. It's something that happens to you while you're immersed in serving your customer."

- Register products as soon after the purchase as possible.

- If an issue occurs and you need to contact the company, keep a record of the following:

  ✓ Date of contact

  ✓ Whom you talked to, including pertinent information such as employee name, identification number, and phone and extension number

  ✓ Details of what was discussed

  ✓ Details of the promised follow-up and timing

- Always communicate facts. Don't call names, make threats or become overly emotional. It is, however, acceptable to be very assertive.

- If a serious problem occurs and you need to write to the company, provide fully detailed information in chronological sequence, including people's names, titles, promised follow-up, account numbers, and your detailed contact information, including your address, phone, fax and e-mail. Don't communicate in generalities.

  Begin your letter with your purpose for writing: "The purpose of this letter is to _____."

  Immediately after stating the purpose of your letter, state specifically what you are looking for. Several examples:

  ✓ I am writing to seek a refund on our _____.

  ✓ I am writing to be reimbursed for _____.

  ✓ I would like our frequent flyer miles reinstated.

✓ I would like a day's credit applied, since my cable was out on (date).

- Following this, create a subhead titled "Background" and explain in chronological sequence what had happened to date. Be as specific and unemotional as possible.

- Always write to the CEO. It may not help, but it won't hurt either. As a former officer of a Fortune 150 company, whenever I received a consumer complaint that was directed to the CEO's office and handed down to me, my objective was to make sure the only reason that consumer would write back to the CEO was to let him know how happy he was with my fast and complete response.

- If the company makes a settlement offer, be reasonable. Think through in advance what makes sense from its perspective and yours, and where you're willing to compromise.

If you become involved in negotiation, reduce your requirements in baby steps, not major increments. For example, if you were looking for $100 in compensation and the company has offered $50, don't come down to $60. It's better to put forward a counteroffer of, say, $90 or $95 if the company will agree to settle your issue right away.

If you haven't yet stated specifically what you are looking for the company to give you, and it asks what you want, let the company bid first. Follow this rule: Never bid against yourself. Ask, "What do you feel is reasonable?" The company might suggest more than you expected. If not, then you can begin your negotiation. For example, you ask, "What do you feel is reasonable?" It says $50, but you feel $80 is more appropriate. Clearly state you feel $100 is reasonable and bargain from there, in small steps.

Try to bargain with something that has value to you and isn't as costly to the company. For example, airlines and hotels will give you miles or frequent-traveler credits faster than cash. It costs the company less, and your usage ensures it will get more business. Stores would prefer to give you an in-store credit.

- When contacting a company, give it at least 30 days to respond. We use a follow-up system to "tickle" the last letter 31 days in advance. If we haven't heard anything, we send another letter, telling the company we're following up. We frequently include the original letter, so it has all the background in case it has "misplaced" the original. Any company that doesn't respond within a month is demonstrating poor customer service.

- If your situation is reasonably serious, copy appropriate regulatory groups, trade groups such as the Better Business Bureau, and governmental agencies, such as your state's attorney general. Most organizational leaders want to avoid negative publicity.

Employees can't be expected to provide excellent customer service with broken tools and lack of training.

Chapter 3

Customer Service Is Always in Style

THIS chapter is directed at business leaders, from shop owners in Paducah, Kentucky, to business executives of major corporations on Park Avenue in New York. If you're "just" a consumer, you're going to enjoy reading this also!

First, Mr., Mrs. or Ms. Business Executive, let's be honest. Especially you big-time corporate executives who get upset when the dinner selection your staff has provided on your G550 corporate jet wasn't prepared properly. For consumers reading this chapter, a G550 is one of handful of decked-out, expensive business jets. G5 is short for Gulfstream 500; go to www.gulfstream.com/g550 to check it out. It has a range of 6,750 nautical miles, cruising at Mach .885 at 51,000 feet. There is now a G650. These "Greyhound buses" for corporate execs include on-board showers, staterooms, galleys with countertop cooking, exercise bikes, surround-sound entertainment systems, multiple flat-panel video monitors, satellite phones and DIRECTV. Tom flew all over the world on planes like this. Don't feel too sorry for the business executives who have to travel a lot, especially when you are standing in a long queue at the airport waiting to get through security.

Now, be honest about the amount of time you, the business leader, seriously paid attention to customer service in the past 12 months. If you did focus on it, it was likely due to a crisis that needed your immediate attention. We're not talking about the short-term, reactionary time you may have invested. We're talking about customer service as a strategy to drive business results. We're talking about a strategy that backs up platitudes such as "our customers come first" or "our customers are our most important asset" or "we're not satisfied until our customers are." This would include all the large banking, cable and cell phone companies — a lot of "happy talk" with poor customer service delivery.

Certainly, there are a number of organizations that have created outstanding customer service strategies and have backed them up with an appropriate level of resources. Some names that come to mind are Four Seasons Hotels and Resorts, Lands' End, Sears, Victoria's Secret, L.L.Bean, 1-800 CONTACTS and Chico's clothing stores. We're sure there are many others. Why do we like these?

Four Seasons Hotels and Resorts

In a following section, we discuss why we think Four Seasons is the best at customer service, so we won't repeat ourselves. We feel it has the best, most consistent customer service.

Lands' End

Lands' End makes it easy to order and has a world-class Web site. It also has people readily available online to answer questions. We've enjoyed shopping with Lands' End because we know if we have any issue at all, the company will gladly take back merchandise. It makes the return process as easy as the purchase process.

Sears

You may not expect Sears to be on our list of the best, but Sears was built on 100 percent customer satisfaction. As kids, we loved going to Sears. It was vibrant and alive, with lots of things to look at. We loved the dishwashers with the clear fronts, where we could watch the water jets. While it's true Sears isn't what it used to be, the Craftsman guarantee keeps us coming back. Why would we buy tools anywhere else? It has great tools, innovations, the Craftsman name and the Sears guarantee. It if breaks for any reason, it gets replaced, no questions asked. We tested the guarantee in the recent past, and it's as good as it ever was.

"Being on par in terms of price and quality only gets you into the game.
Service wins the game."

L.L.Bean

L.L.Bean answers the phone right away. The company has enough people, and they know it's you who's calling and have account numbers on hand. L.L.Bean also embraces technology. When your order arrives, you are provided with two labels: One is postage paid and the company subtracts that from your account for convenience; the other label is preaddressed and you can pay the postage. They make it convenient and give you options.

1-800 CONTACTS

This is an organization that markets, well, contacts. When you call, someone answers right away. It seems to have avoided the queuing nightmare that most companies put consumers through. Moreover, the employees speak clearly, enunciate and demonstrate proper phone etiquette. We're all for cost savings, but if you hire people whom your customers can't understand or who don't have excellent phone etiquette, you may be doing yourself more harm than good.

For example, if you're dealing with people who are hard of hearing, avoid hiring women with higher-pitched voices. The fact is the pitch of many women's voices can be difficult to discern for those hard of hearing. Add to that someone who speaks rapidly and uses "like" and "so," and it can be challenging and annoying to your customers. And let's face it, baby boomers are getting older and hard of hearing (perhaps from too many rock concerts). By the way, don't refer to boomers as "seniors"; they don't appreciate it.

Back to 1-800 CONTACTS. During a phone conversation, its representatives frequently use your name and repeat back your request, to check for understanding. For example, a customer service representative might say, "OK, Mr. Wilson, to make sure I understand, you'd like to return your contacts for a full refund. Is that correct?" For a return, the company sends you a return label that includes postage, and that's all there is to that.

Chico's

Chico's is a woman's clothing store that obviously wants to keep its frequent shoppers coming back. Once a person spends $500, she becomes a Passport Club member. Members receive their catalogs and promotional information automatically by mail and are invited to parties and events. They even have special gifts for Passport Members throughout the year. Shipping is waived and members receive a 5 percent discount.

As mentioned, we're sure there are countless other great examples, and we'd love to hear about them. We're sure there are many individuals who strive to provide outstanding customer service. It's challenging to work in an organization where the process, training and systems don't allow employees to consistently deliver.

12 Success Criteria: Customer Service As a Business Driver

Following are the "12 Commandments" for driving business results by leveraging customer service. We will later discuss each one in detail.

1. Customer service must be established as a core business driver.

2. Senior management must lead and actively support it.

3. The strategy must be long-term in nature — be "inculturated."

4. It must become an organizational expectation.

5. It must be a serious component of performance reviews.

6. Your customer service strategy should be differentiated.

7. You should quantify your position. And the competition's.

8. Set short-, medium- and longer-term objectives.

9. Quantitatively measure results annually.

10. Report progress to employees frequently.

11. Invest in customer service, such as people, tools and systems.

12. Reward employees with recognition, rewards and promotions.

Let's look at each of these in more detail.

Establish Customer Service as a Core Business Driver

All businesses seek to invest time and money in developing a sustainable advantage vs. their competition. Two obvious choices are in product innovation and price. Both require investment in different areas. We'd all love to have our products or services locked up with long-term patents. However, after 30 years of working in consumer products with two world-class companies, this is difficult to nearly impossible to accomplish. There are simply too many smart competitors that can figure out how to design around your intellectual property. Having said that, occasionally companies do develop strong protection.

Another competitive strategy is price. Wal-Mart was built on this foundation from day one. It kept its overhead lower than the competition's and changed the world's retail landscape. Unless you've built your organization from the ground up with a low-cost strategy, you're not likely to become low cost anytime soon. We mentioned previous examples of companies that attempted to compete on price without a low-cost position and lost. Kmart almost went out of business, and Midwest ended up on the airline junk heap with Eastern, Pam Am, TWA and others.

Most executives, when seeking competitive advantage, don't consider customer service. Maybe because it's not glamorous ("Oh, we have to have that, but we try to keep costs down"). Maybe they don't strongly consider it because they didn't teach it in business school and Harvard Business

Review doesn't publish case studies on it. We feel customer service will become the next big "discovery" in driving successful, profitable growth. All the leading business school professors and Blue Chip Consultants will claim to have discovered the key to business growth. It will be the next big buzzword, like the overused "consumer insights."

Business goes through phases, trends and fashion, just like clothing styles and music. For example, at one point it was fashionable to be vertically integrated. If you made cars, you owned ore mines. If you made paper, you owned forests. Today the opposite is true. Today's fashion statement: If it isn't a core competency, it's outsourced. Remember the American Automobile Association example we mentioned? The pendulum will swing back, and organizations will discover customer service as a way to differentiate their brands.

The great thing about developing customer service as a differentiator is that it can't be created overnight. You might ask why that is great. Because it's somewhat of a subversive competitive weapon. For example, if you drop your price, your competition hears about it, usually from your customers, and they can follow you almost immediately. With customer service as a differentiator, by the time it begins having a noticeable impact on your business results, it would take your competitors years to catch up. As a strategy, it's sustainable and ownable. It's an equity builder. And it's measurable, which we'll discuss later.

What makes it great also makes it problematic. Today's business executives seem to have Attention Deficit Disorder. This is brought on by the need to create instant results so they can demonstrate action at the next board meeting. That makes it challenging to "sell" a strategy that may need a couple of years to begin showing results. On the flip side, your competition would be faced with a similar uphill battle. If you capture the high ground before they do, it's less likely they will want to simply copy you.

Senior Management Must Lead and Drive Customer Service

Customer service as a long-term strategy to drive results and differentiate the organization is not something that can be led from the bottom up. Lower- to middle-level management can recommend it, but like anything in an organization, to be successful it must have not only the support of senior management, but they must lead and drive it.

They must communicate the vision, why it's important and how the organization will get there. It can't be seen as another "one off" short-term program developed by management only to be replaced by another a year from now or next quarter.

The Strategy Must Be Long-Term in Nature

Driving business results through customer service is not a short-term program. It's not the annual "drive for success" program. It is a strategy that is well thought out, designed to create a major and sustainable competitive advantage over time. It may take several years before you begin to see tangible results.

It doesn't have to be a big-bang program. It can be implemented in phases to better manage cash flow, allowing you to learn as you go and make adjustments to fit your particular business or industry — big or small, in any industry.

It Must Become an Organizational Expectation

All employees must be aware that:

- The focus on customer service is a major organizational strategy. Ideally, they first hear about it from senior management.

- The company is investing in it, with people, training, processes and systems.

- Each employee will play a role and will know what his or hers is.

- Results will be measured and reported on a regular basis.

- Employee contribution to customer service will be evaluated annually as part of a performance review.

It Must Be a Serious Component of Performance Reviews

We included the word "serious" because so often companies include accountabilities in position descriptions without any teeth. For example, we've seen statements such as "support corporate diversity and inclusivity efforts." That doesn't say much, is open to interpretation, and typically in reviews may not be covered or is merely glossed over. Therefore, the word serious means there will be a serious discussion of an employee's contribution, or lack thereof, to help reach specific customer service objectives.

Differentiate Your Customer Service Strategy

You need to understand what is important to your customers and design your customer service strategy to meet those needs better than anyone else. Just like companies strive to position their products and services to be unique and distinctive, you need to do the same with customer service. Remember the CenterBrain Three T's we're sharing below. As previously mentioned, The CareGiver Partnership positioned its business on providing Personalized Attention^{SM} service with specific elements of how our differentiated level of service is delivered.

*T*angible Benefit

Your customer service selling proposition should quickly answer the consumer's question of, "What's in it for me?" In the case of Sears Craftsman tools, the benefit is value. I know if I buy a tool and anything goes wrong at any time for any reason, I get a new one with no questions asked.

*T*ruth

Support for the selling proposition is grounded in logic. The guarantee on Sears Craftsman tools is backed — the company delivers on the claim. No ifs, ands or buts; no mouse type, legalese, exceptions or disclaimers.

*T*hat's Me

A universal insight is acknowledged that lets the consumer or customer know your organization understands him better than any other. Sears knows its customers shop for value. A 100 percent lifetime guarantee spells value to the consumer.

Quantify Your Position, and the Competition's

Develop a quantified baseline understanding of how your important customer groups rate doing business with you. Include the competition. Think through your questionnaire so it can be used long into the future and trends can be monitored. When you measure performance, use a quintile measurement of your customers so you get input from a cross section of your largest to your smallest customers.

Set Short-, Medium- and Longer-Term Objectives

Once you know what the baseline is, establish short-, medium- and long-term targets. Identify the strategy you will employ to achieve those objectives. Further break down key milestones and resources that will be required. This includes incremental head count, improved training, and systems and tools.

"Choose to deliver amazing service to your customers. You'll stand out because they don't get it anywhere else."

43

Quantitatively Measure Results on an Ongoing Basis

Conduct a tracking study to measure progress on a regular basis. Include the competition. Without this tool, you will not know if you are making progress. You may develop some areas more quickly than others and decide to place more resources against objectives that are progressing more slowly that you'd like. A book on this that we embrace is titled "The Ultimate Question." We recommend reading it and getting copies for those within your organization.

At The CareGiver Partnership, we continually track our Net Promoter Score, or NPS. A company's NPS is a concept from the aforementioned "The Ultimate Question" by Fred Reichheld of Bain & Company. His premise is that companies that provide excellent service have higher margins, grow faster and make more money. To measure this, we employ an outside third-party market research organization that mails surveys to customers who have purchased from us at least two times. One of the questions asked is, "Based on your personal experience with The CareGiver Partnership, how likely would you be to recommend us to a family member or friend?" We use a scale from 1 to 10, with 10 being "highly likely." Consumers who rate us a 1 through 6 (detractors) are subtracted from those rating us a 9 or 10 (promoters); the net result is our NPS, which ranges from 85 to 90+ percent. Financial institutions we've consulted for often have a negative NPS; they have lots of customers that really, really dislike them. Our guess is that most banks, credit card brands, cable companies and cell phone providers would have a negative NPS.

Report Progress to Employees Frequently

Include updates of customer service in all key meeting and communication vehicles throughout your organization. Don't give a presentation without discussing progress on customer service, what areas need improvement and what future investments are planned.

At The CareGiver Partnership, customer input from our tracking study is entered weekly into an online database. Results are available online for all at The CareGiver Partnership to read. In this manner, it isn't "management" telling the team what needs to be enhanced, because the team can see what consumers are saying each week and make adjustments.

Invest in Customer Service

All the greatest strategies, consultants' recommendations and quantified studies are worthless without an investment in customer service. The key investments are people, tools and systems. Let's review each.

People

People are at the heart of driving your customer service results. There are four people components:

- Sufficient quantity
- High quality, intelligent and motivated
- In-depth and ongoing training
- Empowered

Sufficient Quantity

The most highly trained people supported with the best systems can't get the job done if there aren't sufficient numbers. For example, in a call center on Monday morning, if you need 12 people on the phones to cover the weekend buildup and you only have eight, you're going to have poor results. This happens frequently. Companies know Monday's call volume is the highest of any day in the week, yet they allow consumers to act as the "governor," a term we previously defined in the context of customer service. Rather than having enough people to take your call, you hear, "Due to a higher than normal call volume, your wait will be at least XX minutes."

Worse yet is, "Due to higher than normal call volume, you should call back later." Click.

At The CareGiver Partnership, we have more people on the phones on Mondays so we can answer all calls by the third ring. The other peak period is between 10 a.m. and 2 p.m., while people are on lunch breaks from the East Coast to the West Coast.

The bottom line is, you need people in sufficient numbers. If there is downtime, employees can conduct training or learn about new or improved products, features or problem areas. Don't make your customers queue up and listen to annoying recorded music. Even worse for a customer is being placed on hold and being forced to listen to someone who sounds like he is on amphetamines telling you how important customer service is to the company, or that the company won the J.D. Power award last year for great service. We swear executives don't call their own customer service areas. If they did, many would be incensed and make immediate changes.

Following is an example of listening to and responding to consumers' service needs. At CenterBrain Partners, we consulted with a leading manufacturer of playground equipment. The particular product was sold at stores like Home Depot and Lowe's. Through our research, which included listening to consumers, we learned that for most men (and yes, it's the men who typically construct these), building a play set is not easy. We also learned the company had a customer service hot line to provide help Mondays through Fridays. The problem was that most men construct play sets on weekends. The company completely redesigned the build system, eliminating more than half the parts and steps. It also had its customer service team available on weekends during the spring and summer, with product engineers on call for the really tough questions.

Quality

The second people component is quality. You have to hire good people with valuable backgrounds, who are intelligent, articulate and can speak English, or the language you communicate in. If your customer service people can't be understood by your customers, you might be doing more harm than good. There is a saying Tom heard in a presentation from the CEO of Wal-Mart: "You can train skills, but you can't train attitude. Hire people with good attitudes." We agree completely.

Training

The third people aspect is training, to which there are two parts. The first includes in-depth training in your products or services. So often we're confronted with customer service people who obviously don't know the product line. Worse are companies that outsource customer service. The people who represent them may not know much about the company itself, let alone the particulars of the product or service. We have a real problem with outsourcing customer service; if you are serious about customer service, you simply wouldn't do this. We believe your customer service people should be more knowledgeable about your product or service than your customers. This just makes sense. You must give your customer service people sample products to take home, and use if practical. You should also include your competitors' products.

The second part of training is to enhance certain skill sets. The three most important skills are communications, negotiations and conflict resolution. There are many good sources for each of these. For example, in the area of negotiating, there is an audio CD set we think is particularly good; its title is "The Power of Nice."

Earlier we mentioned customer service organizations must be properly staffed, and that downtime can be used for training and other tasks. In this case, during a slower period, an employee could put on headphones and listen to a training CD. The benefits are zero wasted time, enhanced skill sets, improved customer service and reduced boredom.

Empowerment

The fourth people aspect is empowerment. You shouldn't tie your customer service people to a policy manual or a script. They need to understand and internalize the organizational vision and act accordingly, on their own. As previously mentioned, Lynn worked for Dayton's, which begat Marshall Field's, which begat Macy's. At one point, Field's decided to empower the associates and let them resolve issues right on the spot without checking with a manager. We thought this made great sense. It certainly made the employees feel more important and trusted, and the customers didn't have to wait around for approvals from a manager.

Unfortunately, there was little "constancy of purpose" as Dayton's became Field's, then Macy's. Customer service strategies have changed with each new regime, leaving employees disillusioned and customers confused. Same-store sales at Macy's plunged by more than 5 percent during the 2009 fiscal year. To make ends meet, they've cut customer service differentiators, such as free gift wrapping, parcel pickup, a rewards program for its best customers, sending an item from one store to another at no charge, and cutting head count. They are embarking on a similar strategy that bankrupted Kmart and put Midwest out of business. Instead, the company's energy should be spent creating a positioning of highly differentiated customer service, the hallmark of department stores.

We believe that when you empower employees, they will resolve issues at a lower cost than tying them to a policy manual developed at corporate headquarters by individuals who aren't as close to the customer. We can't prove this and we're not aware of any empirical evidence to suggest the contrary; we simply believe that properly recruited, trained and empowered employees will result in more customers staying with you over the long term.

Tools

As mentioned, the three investments required in order to create excellent customer service are people, tools and systems. We reviewed the four components of the people investment, and now we'll review the tools.

Think of tools in the context of farming. If you ask a farmer to grow and harvest corn, he needs the proper tools to be successful. This may include seed, fertilizer, water and a combine. You wouldn't expect him to get the job done without the proper tools.

Your customer service people need tools in just the same way. The tools may vary depending on the circumstances, but may include appropriate workspaces, computers, customer databases, PDAs, cell phones, global positioning systems, calculators, vehicles and parts. Think about the service person that shows up late to your house without the right parts to repair your washing machine. The company didn't stock the van properly and didn't provide a map or GPS to help locate your home.

On a business trip to New York, Tom landed at LaGuardia and hopped in a cab to Great Neck Long Island. As he approached Great Neck, the driver pulled into a gas station for directions, and then drove around for another 15 minutes before pulling into a second station for directions. A $150 GPS would have allowed him to make more money by not wasting his time — Tom didn't pay him for his mistakes — and he would have had a happier customer. We realize that New York City taxi drivers aren't known for customer service.

Tools improve employee morale and confidence, reduce stress and improve efficiency. We are always surprised today when a service rep, or taxi or limo driver, asks, "How do I get to your home?" We want to say, "Have you heard of Google, or an inexpensive portable GPS system?"

Systems

The final investment is systems. Let's begin with an example. When you call L.L.Bean and the phone is answered right away by a pleasant-sounding, articulate person, you know that L.L.Bean has hired a sufficient number of well-recruited and trained people.

The person you are speaking to already has your account and purchase history, because the company's computer system ties the customer database with caller ID. As soon as you call, the computer looks up your phone number in its database and presents the customer service representative with your account information and purchase history. Impressive. That's systems.

Think about the experience if the customer service representative had to ask your name, put you on hold and toggle through paper or computer records to find your information. It just wouldn't be the same. It would also be much less efficient for L.L.Bean, which would need additional employees to manage the inefficiency.

Our biggest concern with systems is they frequently are installed for the wrong reasons. In other words, systems should *support* your customer service, not replace it. A phone queuing system that forces consumers to push buttons and make multiple choices is an example of a system that supplants good customer service. The only reason it was installed was to save the company money by taking customer calls, forcing them to make multiple choices, then parking them on hold until someone becomes available to take their calls, which is what we refer to as forcing the customer to be the governor rather than having a sufficient number of employees available to personally answer calls.

"Customers are an investment. Maximize your return."

Have you ever contacted your credit card company? Usually you are asked to enter your card number or some other identification. You then wait on hold, until the first thing you're asked is, "May I have your credit card number?" What happened to the one you entered? If you are transferred to someone else, the process starts over again; it's kind of like playing Chutes and Ladders. Maybe that is the reason they have a negative Net Promoter Score, meaning more people dislike than like their service. They don't really care that much. Large banks and credit card companies generally are not your friend. Where possible, always support your local bank or credit union.

Recognize and Reward Employees

Acknowledgement. This is so important. Acknowledgement or recognition is free and is used so infrequently. This always astounds us. If you want to focus employees on enhancing customer service, make sure you acknowledge and recognize excellent results. It doesn't have to be done with prizes, promotions or cash; it can be as simple as a letter from a leader or recognition during a meeting. If employees don't feel like it's important to you as a leader, it won't be important to them.

"Eugh!!"

"I know your new couch was supposed to
be delivered two weeks ago, but the
factory is running **behind**."

Chapter 4
The Four Bad Words

THERE are four words you need to be on the lookout for when dealing with a company. They are "behind," "should," "shortly" and "try." Let's look at each.

Behind

"I know your new couch was supposed to be delivered two weeks ago, but the factory is running behind." The fact that they are running behind is not your problem; it is a problem with their planning, their process, their execution or a combination of all. They didn't plan enough people to work that day, they didn't plan to have the right parts available for the service person, or they didn't plan enough time for the previous jobs. For all you know, the service person overslept and you are making up for it by being forced to stay home and wait.

Should

This word is of no value to you. How many times have you heard it in these contexts?

He should be there …

He should have adjusted, fixed, checked …

Normally, he should ask you if …

He should have called you …

He should have checked for damage before …

He should have been there on time …

Shortly

This is similar to "should." Ask 10 people to define how many minutes are in the word "shortly." The problem with this word, when you hear it from an organization, is that it doesn't tell you anything.

When told, "He should be there shortly," you should ask exactly when he will arrive. If the individual can't tell you, start with a 15-minute window: "OK, if you can't tell me when he will be here, can you tell me if he will be here between now (assuming 1 p.m.) and 1:15? The point is that your time is valuable, possibly more valuable on a per-hour basis than theirs. They are stealing this time from you and using you as the governor for their poor planning and ineptness. What's worse is they couldn't care less. No one's looking out for you but you.

Try

To us, this is a weasel word, meaning that whatever they are going to try and do probably isn't going to happen. But by using the word in an almost legalistic sense, the person using it can't be held accountable when she doesn't come through for you.

Following are three examples:

We had ordered one computer, and the company shipped two complete systems and a third CPU. Naturally, we called to have the incorrect systems picked up. We were told the company would "try" to have them picked up.

On another occasion, after noticing some vinyl siding on our house had faded, we contacted the manufacturer. The company sent a service representative, who took photos. After not hearing anything for some time, we contacted the manufacturer again. The service representative said he would "try" to locate the photos. This was code for he didn't know where they were.

The final example was with a major airline. While on a trip, Lynn called the customer service number first thing on a Monday morning to confirm a return flight home. She received a recorded message saying that due to heavy call volume, she should "try" calling back later and then the phone disconnected. She tried repeatedly, but to no avail.

"Try" allows companies and employees to feel good that they at least tried. Companies, who are the best at customer service, don't try; they deliver. Consistently.

Throughout the book, we have put quotation marks around each of these aforementioned words so you can see firsthand how they are used by organizations in the context of communicating to consumers by mail, over the phone or via e-mail.

FOUR SEASONS
Hotels and Resorts

L.L.Bean

1 800 CONTACTS ®

Sears

chico's

LANDS' END

Chapter 5

The Customer Service Gold Standard

WE have been extremely fortunate to be able to enjoy staying in the best hotel chain in the world, The Four Seasons. When Tom worked at Kimberly-Clark, it was the hotel of choice because it was the CEO's favorite. Besides being the best in the world, it is one of the best customer service organizations.

Anyone can build great hotels with comfortable beds and five-diamond restaurants. The trick is, how you get everyone, and we mean everyone, to deliver world-class service, from the hotel manager to the gardeners, porters and wait staff.

We've stayed in at least six of its properties, including Maui, Mexico City, Puerto Rico, Austin, Dallas and Chicago. They have what it takes to deliver — a sufficient number of intelligent, highly trained and empowered employees. Intelligence doesn't mean having an IQ of 150; it means having common sense in dealing with people face to face. Training is critical to ensure everyone lives and breathes what the company is about — its DNA, brand essence, the advertising that we see.

We remember once being on a shuttle van, going to pick up our rental car at an airport. The driver had a boombox going full tilt and was talking with an off-duty friend, who was sitting on the floor next to her, smoking a cigarette. This company's advertising slogan came to mind: "We Try Harder." Better keep trying. This wouldn't happen if they had hired employees who knew better. If Four Seasons can do it, so can your organization.

Referring back to the steps required to create an excellent customer service driven organization, we'd like to spend some time reinforcing the

"Customers don't expect you to be perfect.
They do expect you to fix things when they go wrong."

critical importance of investing in people, tools and systems. This is so important because these are the people your customers see and talk to day in and day out.

As an executive, you may wear $1,000 suits, have an MBA from Harvard and use all the latest buzzwords, but the bottom line is that your customers will never or rarely come into contact with you personally. They interface with your front line people. For example, during a 10-day stay in Maui, we saw many servers, groundskeepers and reservationists, but we never saw the general manager. We're sure that he (we know it was a he) is an excellent employee, but it was the front line people that created the impression we have of Four Seasons Maui. Anyone can buy expensive properties and build hotels and resorts with lots of marble. The trick is pulling it all together with great customer service. And that starts with people.

You have to start by hiring great people, people who possess great attitudes. You must pay them well and quit worrying about how much extra they cost vs. the outsourced option. We've already explained why this is so important to your brand equity. You have to hire and staff in sufficient numbers. Invest in ongoing training so they know your product or service and expectations better than your customers.

It's necessary to train your employees in specific skill areas, such as communication, negotiation and conflict resolution. Empower them to make-on-the-spot, binding decisions. We don't mean "empowerment" as it's used on a company's Web site or brochure; we mean real empowerment, where you trust your employees to make decisions on your behalf. Provide them with the tools they need to do their jobs. Last, you have to support their efforts with systems — the high-tech part of the high touch.

"Just because I said you could return it,
doesn't mean you can actually return it."

Chapter 6
How It All Began: The Sting

THE following pages include a number of actual issues we've encountered over the years. The purpose is to illustrate common customer service issues that cost you time and money. More importantly, we hope to provide you with tools to help you successfully negotiate in your favor so you get your money's worth as a consumer.

We sometimes think we must be possessed, because we seem to run into so many issues dealing with various organizations — manufacturers, service personnel, financial institutions, medical providers and even nonprofits. We are nice people and have normal expectations. We've never been out to get something for nothing. However, we've always taken the time to attempt to get our money's worth, to get what was promised. Along the way, we discovered there are many people who, when confronted with poor service, just say, "Oh well, that's the way it goes."

This situation really upset us and still does to this day. Sometimes you have to fight fire with fire, especially after having tried logic and reason. During the late 1970s, before Game Boy, Sony PlayStation and Microsoft Xbox, Atari was the king of the game systems. Lynn decided to buy a game for her brother for Christmas. We were visiting her parents in Naperville, Illinois, in December 1978 and bought the game from a family-owned business in a large shopping mall in Aurora. Before purchasing it, Lynn asked the owner if it could be returned, as she was buying it as a gift. He said that would be no problem as long as it wasn't opened and she had a receipt.

Her brother received two of the same game. Lynn went to the store to return it, game in hand, unopened, along with the receipt. When she explained the situation to the owner, he flat out said his store didn't accept returns. She reminded him of the conversation they had when he sold it to her. It was as if it never happened. Frustrated, she drove back to her parents' house and explained what happened. Time for plan B. This time, her brother went to the store and attempted to exchange, not return, it. Wasn't going to happen. He left the store and came home with the game.

We wondered how a business person could be so deceitful. Tom happened to be on vacation — we were living in New Jersey — and had time to kill. He thought about what it was going to take to deal with this guy. After giving it a great deal of thought, the light bulb went off. The movie "The Sting" was still fresh in our minds, having been released about five years earlier. Tom decided we needed to pull a sting on this guy.

The first thing Tom did was write three letters, one each to American Express, the Better Business Bureau and the chamber of commerce. Then we went to the shopping mall. Walking by the store, Lynn pointed out the person she had dealt with. Tom nonchalantly walked into the store, which was rather busy, and searched out the most expensive television, making sure it wasn't one that was on sale. We figured Mr. Owner would take the bait of a potential sale of a high-ticket, high-margin item, in much the same way the piranhas used to attack the goldfish at the Ace Hardware where Tom grew up in Naperville.

It worked as planned. "Can I help you?" the owner said politely. Acting like Detective Columbo and coming off a bit aloof, Tom explained he was visiting his in-laws, it was their 25th wedding anniversary and he wanted to get them a nice TV. "Is this a good TV?" he asked. Not only was it his best, it was loaded with profit for him. Tom let him "sell" him and said he'd take it, but that he would have to arrange delivery later. After he rung up the TV, and just before signing the charge receipt, Tom pulled out the Atari game and asked for a refund. He provided a full cash refund on the spot. Tom signed the charge receipt and left the store.

When we returned to Lynn's parents' house about half an hour later, Tom phoned the store and asked for the owner. He explained who he was and was greeted in a very friendly tone. "What can I do for you, Tom?" he asked. Tom explained the situation regarding his deceptive practices and told him we had no intention of taking delivery of the TV. "Furthermore," Tom said, "we've already sent letters to American Express, the Better Business Bureau and the chamber of commerce, exposing your business practices." His only response was, "Well, I guess you got me."

It is unbelievable to us that a business owner would risk his reputation like that. We don't recommend being devious, but in this case, we were left with no other options.

"There we go. Perfect."

Chapter 7

Loss of a 25-Year Loyal Customer

THIS is an example of how a well-known, respected company can take a loyal, heavy-buying customer and end a 25-year relationship. What makes this most startling is that it involved the CEO of one of the most respected furniture manufacturers and the owner of two of its dealerships. The name, which most people will recognize, was Ethan Allen.

Sometime during his late teens, Tom became aware of the Ethan Allen brand through his sister. She was married and had been purchasing pieces of its Early American distressed-pine line. His older brother began purchasing the same after he returned from serving in Vietnam.

Into our early 20s, we developed a respect for the brand. Its construction was outstanding, with dovetail drawers, excellent finishes, and, most importantly, well-merchandised and well-staffed galleries.

Our first Ethan Allen gallery experience was in St. Charles, Illinois. We were engaged to be married and had purchased Tom's brother's house about six months before the big day. Having recently graduated from college, we naturally didn't own any furniture to speak of.

The Carriage House Ethan Allen in St. Charles had a "lemon shop" that was open only on Saturdays until noon. It sold returned merchandise that was either in perfect condition or only slightly marred. We made a point of visiting it on many Saturdays, looking for items that might meet our needs. We also chose the Early American line of pine, because that was what Tom's sister and brother were buying and, at the time, it was in style.

"It helps a ton when you learn people's names and
don't butcher them when trying to pronounce them."

65

We really looked forward to those visits because we systematically began collecting a piece here and a piece there. Even though we had little money and were young, the store treated us with dignity and respect. The policy we appreciated most was its approach to payment. The first time we made a purchase, the clerk asked for our name and address and said the store would bill us, no identification required. It also had a policy of not invoicing for at least 90 days with no interest. This was well before the days of "no pay for a year," where retailers sell your credit to a finance company, hoping you won't be able to make the payment when it's due so they can collect a hefty interest payment.

After our first purchase at the Carriage House, we were only asked for our names. This was only occasionally, as a number of the staff began to recognize us. This is a determined strategy that organizations like the Four Seasons, some cruise ships and Disney employ; they work at learning your name, tastes and needs. It doesn't just happen by itself; it's part of their strategy.

For example, on a 10-day stay at the Four Seasons in Maui in February 2003, we were greeted at breakfast by our names after being there for a few days. Another example: Tom attended a presentation at Disney in Orlando on how the company works to provide the best customer service. He learned that when a family enters the park, Disney obtains their names and the resort they're staying at, and then phones ahead to alert the resort staff so they can welcome them by their names. Nice touch!

Another Disney example is every night at park closing, there are a few people who, in all the excitement of the day, can't recall where they parked. People often panic when they realize how many vehicles the lots hold. Disney developed a process to manage this: Since it parks visitors by section, when a guest requests help finding a vehicle, the staff simply asks what time they arrived and can direct them to the location of their vehicle because they keep a daily record. "Ah, you're parked in Mickey row 22." Another nice customer service touch, and there are many others.

For those of you who have cruised, you quickly realize the wait staff and attendants work really hard to learn your name and tastes. After day two, they have you down.

The Carriage House Ethan Allen in St. Charles provided this personalized customer service and made us feel they really appreciated our business.

After we were married, we made a major acquisition with money given to us as wedding gifts. This purchase wasn't from the "lemon shop," however. It was first line merchandise and it was expensive — a triple dresser with top for $900 in 1976, which was about $3,300+ in 2009. That was a major investment for us, but we felt it was worth the money because of the quality that could last a lifetime. The gallery personnel were also a driving force that brought us back again and again.

For the next 25 years, we collected additional pieces as we moved from Illinois to New Jersey to Wisconsin, then down to Texas and back to Wisconsin. Throughout this time period, we had good experiences with the various galleries we did business with. None, however, compared to the "Four Seasons" of galleries, The Carriage House in St. Charles.

After being a loyal customer and heavy buyer for 25 years, it all came to an abrupt end. The attached series of correspondence between us, the CEO of Ethan Allen and the owner of our local gallery will provide the background for why this happened. It is also the first example of how to state your case in a letter.

Aug. 4, 1998

Mr. M. Farooq K.
Chairman, President and CEO
Ethan Allen
Ethan Allen Drive
Danbury, CT 06811

Dear Mr. K.:

The purpose of this letter is to share with you our experience with Kitzlarr's Carriage House located in Appleton, Wisconsin (which has since gone out of business). I feel the matter is important enough to write to you, the CEO, directly. I know you are busy; so am I. I promise this matter is worth 10 minutes of your time.

Background

My wife, Lynn, and I have been purchasing Ethan Allen furniture for 25 years. We have lived in a number of areas, including Chicago, New York, Texas and Wisconsin. In each location, we have purchased Ethan Allen furniture — always with a level of service that mirrors the brand equity and image Ethan Allen enjoys.

Our experience is that Kitzlaar's Carriage House in Green Bay and Appleton, Wisconsin — including Pete K. himself — does not live up to this standard. Following is a detailed outline of our experience with three purchases over a three-year period: a sleigh bed, an entertainment center and a curio cabinet.

Feb. 11, 1998

✓ Entertainment center ordered Feb. 11, 1998, in Appleton, Wisconsin, store with designer Sharon.

✓ Order # XXXXXX; account # XXXXXXXX

- ✓ Promised delivery of six to eight weeks.

- ✓ Wilsons provide a deposit of $2,153.70.

- ✓ Sharon volunteers to contact plant and call with ship date.

Mid-March

- ✓ No call received regarding delivery timing.

- ✓ Lynn Wilson contacts store.

March

- ✓ Wilsons' Visa card is incorrectly debited with a Green Bay customer's charge.

- ✓ I called to have debit reversed.

Late March

- ✓ Sharon checks on order.

- ✓ Ship date might be late May, but can't tell for sure.

- ✓ Late May would be 14 weeks vs. the six to eight weeks that had been promised.

April

- ✓ I called Sharon and asked her to either cancel the order or provide a ship date.

- ✓ I also requested that the deposit we were required to make be credited back to our Visa because we shouldn't have to finance Kitzlaar's inventory, especially since a ship date can't be determined.

- ✓ I was told by the Appleton store manager, "We can't remove the charge and you can't cancel your order; the ship date given to you in March is only an estimate."

✓ I called Pete K., store owner, on April 21, 1998. Pete agreed to credit our Visa for the deposit and to also check on the ship date.

✓ To get to this point, I had to talk with Sharon and the manager of the Appleton, Wisconsin, store, who have not been given decision-making authority.

Late April/Early May

✓ Pete contacted me with a ship date of May 25 from the plant. He said it could be delivered as late as mid-June. This would make it 17 weeks from order date.

✓ I agreed in good faith not to cancel the order. I also agreed to take delivery when it finally arrived, even though a custom-made cabinet could have been built locally in less time.

Late May

✓ I received three contacts regarding delivery timing: one from the Appleton store and two from contract delivery people.

✓ I rearranged our schedule to meet the contract movers' preferred delivery timing, as they only deliver once per week.

May 26

✓ Delivery was scheduled to take place between 4:30 and 6:30 p.m. I left work early in order to accept delivery.

✓ At 6:45 p.m., the contract delivery people still hadn't arrived or phoned. I called the store to find out the status.

✓ The delivery people finally arrived at 7 p.m. They didn't know how to assemble the furniture, so they left the work undone.

✓ I was told that Scott from contract movers will contact me the following day, May 27.

May 27

- ✓ I called Scott twice, at 8 a.m. and 6 p.m., to set up a time for him to stop by. I talked with Scott's wife, who told me Scott would call me back in the evening.

- ✓ I explained to Scott's wife that I had arranged to have people come to hook up all the stereo components in the entertainment center and they couldn't be called off. I needed the entertainment center be set up no later than Thursday evening.

- ✓ Scott did not return our call that evening as promised.

May 28

- ✓ I called Pete to explain the situation.

- ✓ Pete said he would contact the delivery people and follow up in the evening to assure the cabinet is set up prior to the people arriving at our house to set up the stereo components.

- ✓ The contract movers finally called at 2 p.m. to set up a 5 p.m. appointment. I left work early to meet them.

- ✓ At 7 p.m. the movers hadn't arrived or called. I called to find out where they were, but no one answered the phone. I left a message on the answering machine.

- ✓ At 7 p.m. Pete called to check to make sure the work was done, which it wasn't. I was running an errand and called Pete back within 15 minutes, but he had left for the day and didn't leave a phone number where he could be reached.

- ✓ I was upset and left a message with the expectation that something be done immediately.

- ✓ Eric contacted me from the Green Bay store and agreed to set up the entertainment center himself Friday morning at 8 a.m., just before the people from the electronics store were to arrive.

- ✓ Eric admitted to me that Kitzlaar's had serious problems with its contract movers. In fact, they had customers refuse more than $20,000 of furniture that week alone. Further, Eric told me the store was going to go back to doing its own delivery.

✓ At 8:30 p.m. Thursday night, Scott from the contract movers arrived unannounced and more than three hours late to set up the furniture.

✓ I told him that since no one had contacted me, I had made arrangements directly with Kitzlaar's.

May 29

✓ Eric arrived promptly at our home at 8 a.m. as promised and set up the entertainment center.

✓ Lynn asked Eric to look at an Ethan Allen sleigh bed, which we purchased March 2, 1995. The bed didn't support the mattress and box spring properly.

✓ Eric said the supports were too long and he agreed to order the correct ones.

✓ Lynn contacted Sharon at the Appleton store and ordered a curio cabinet for delivery in 10 to 12 weeks.

July

✓ Lynn called Sharon to see if the correct bed supports were in that Eric promised. Sharon didn't know.

✓ Lynn called Eric about the bed supports and he said he would check and get back to us.

Mid-August

✓ Sharon called Lynn to tell her the curio cabinet would be in soon and she will be contacted for delivery.

Week of Aug. 17

✓ Lynn was contacted about delivery of the curio cabinet and discovered that Kitzlaar's was still using same contract movers that delivered the entertainment center.

"Do what you do so well that they will want to see it again and bring their friends."

✓ It took three weeks to arrange delivery because the contract movers only deliver once per week and they can't guarantee a time.

Sept. 2

✓ The curio cabinet was finally delivered. It was missing the pegs that hold the shelves in place.

✓ Lynn asked the contract movers where the pegs were. They told her they're usually in a bag taped to the top of the unit.

✓ After having the curio cabinet in inventory for three weeks, no one ever checked for the parts.

✓ Lynn called Eric at the Green Bay store. He agreed to deliver the parts to our home himself.

Sept. 3

✓ Eric arrives to deliver the pegs for the curio cabinet and the correct supports for the sleigh bed. He had ordered the bed supports on May 28, more than three months prior.

✓ The new supports for the sleigh bed were the same as the current ones that didn't fit. Eric now said the reason they didn't work is the carpet is too thick or the supports need more time to settle into the carpet.

✓ The room has normal wall-to-wall carpet. Moreover, the bed was purchased in March 1995 and has been "settling" for more than three years.

✓ For the difficulties mentioned above, Pete's judgment was to reduce the price of the curio cabinet by $100, or 7 percent.

Mr. K., your Web site talks about the future of customer service at Ethan Allen:

As we approach the new millennium, our focus on servicing the consumer becomes even more important. In order to stay ahead in the increasingly competitive home furnishings marketplace, we must continue to build our relationship with the consumer, both on a local store and national brand level. To do this, we must take what we have done for the past 65 years and do it even better. We were founded on the philosophy of selling service, not just product. Looking forward, this dedication to the customer will remain at the heart of everything we do.

A study conducted by Technical Assistance Research Programs, Inc. (TARP, which is now an interesting acronym), which was commissioned by the U.S. Department of Consumer Affairs, found:

- Ninety-six percent of consumers won't let you know they are dissatisfied.

- Of these, up to 90 percent won't buy again from your company.

- You can win back up to 70 percent of customers by resolving the problem.

- If you handle problems quickly and well, 95 percent will become loyal customers.

Based on our experiences described above, Kitzlaar's has a long way to go to achieve your vision. As a result, we can't imagine why we would do business with them, and as a consequence, Ethan Allen, going forward. We also feel the employees at Kitzlaar's view Lynn and I as complainers — not a position we enjoy.

Mr. K., I hope the 10 minutes you have invested reading this will provide the impetus to passionately reaffirm the importance of building long-standing customer relationships within your corporate and dealer organizations.

Sincerely,
Tom Wilson
C: Pete K.

Mr. K. responded to our letter and had one of his customer service people send a follow-up letter. The correspondence follows in the next few pages.

In his return letter, he thanked Tom for bringing this to his attention and wrote he was going to review it with his associates. He failed to mention when we should expect to hear something or who will be contacting us. Essentially, this was a letter that did not address the issues at hand.

On Oct. 12, 1998, Ms. F., customer service representative at Ethan Allen corporate, also sent us a letter. After we took the time to fully document a serious problem with the service of one of their galleries five weeks later, Ms. F. also sent us a letter that didn't address the problem.

While she apologized and said she couldn't do anything about what had already happened, as she wasn't empowered, she stated that service is what made Ethan Allen great. As a consumer, I really don't care what made them great; I only care about our situation. The saying "you can't rest on your laurels" fits perfectly here. Don't tell me about the 99 percent of the time you get it right; tell me about what action you're going to take now.

She went on to say that, unfortunately, our situation may not have been indicative of the Ethan Allen image. The words "may not have been" were a gross understatement and an insult, after the time we took to provide the company with detailed, accurate and actionable information.

The Green Bay headquartered carriage house had just botched the service of three orders, totaling more than $8,000, to a 25-year loyal customer and we received two letters that didn't even address the issues, one from its CEO. They allowed their dealer to use untrained, outsourced delivery people who were rude, crude and certainly did not enhance Ethan Allen's brand equity. And to that, Ms. F. tells us our experience "may not be indicative of their image?" Really?

Guess when the last time was when we purchased furniture from Ethan Allen? Friday, May 28, 1998. We have purchased a great deal of high-end furniture since then.

Following is a letter I sent to Ethan Allen's CEO:

Nov. 30, 1998

Mr. M. Farooq K.
Chairman, President and CEO
Ethan Allen

Dear Mr. K.:

This is a follow-up to our letter dated Sept. 8. You replied Sept. 23 and forwarded our comments to Ms. F., who sent me a letter dated Oct. 12.

In Ms. F.'s letter, she indicated Mr. K. "regretted the chain of events that led to our dissatisfaction" and that he would respond to me directly.

It has now been more six weeks since Mr. K. was to follow up with me. He has not, nor has Ms. F. or yourself. I am quite sure of this, as I have voice mail and caller ID.

Since I have waited patiently and did not hear from Mr. K., Ms. F. or yourself, we took it upon ourselves to repair the sleigh bed.

You yourself, Ms. F. and certainly Mr. K. have clearly demonstrated that customer service is not an important issue to Ethan Allen. I am therefore left with no other option but to discontinue purchasing Ethan Allen furniture in the future. We have been loyal customers since 1975.

Sincerely,
Thomas E. Wilson
C: Pete K., Ms. F.

On Dec. 9, 1998, we received a letter from the owner of the local carriage house. This was a full three months since we had written to the Ethan Allen CEO. In it, the owner told us his delay in responding was inexcusable and totally his fault. To his credit, he apologized, telling us the company has had "exemplary customer service for 25 years." He also told us that based on our input, it was eliminating the practice of outsourcing delivery. He ended his letter with another apology, saying, "Should you decide to purchase from us again, I promise you a better experience."

While we appreciated his letter and his elimination of outsourced delivery, he should have done more to try and keep us as a customer. As marketing people, we would want to save a loyal, long-term, highly profitable customer. Don't promise us a better future experience; give us a reason to come back today.

For example, a discount on our current purchase would have been a logical offer. We think this makes good sense and, more importantly, is just good business sense. If you have a bad experience at a restaurant, it may take the charge off your bill or discount it, depending on the circumstances. It doesn't tell you that if you decide to visit again, we'll try and make it better. Why not do the same in a furniture store?

On Dec. 16, 1998, we received a letter from Ethan Allen's consumer affairs manager. It was a follow-up to the owner's letter above, another typical corporate letter. Following are several phrases from it. "We regret the difficulties you encountered." They regret it, but they never apologized for it. "We regret any delay in response." Again, they regret it but don't apologize for it. We also love the phrase "any delay." There wasn't "any delay"; there was a big delay. And finally, "We make every effort to ensure our valued customers get the service and quality that is synonymous with Ethan Allen." That wasn't true, because no one from Ethan Allen corporate,

"Do what you say you're going to do, when you say you're going to do it, in the way you said you were going to do it."

77

including the CEO, did anything except send several form letters. They didn't make every effort; in fact, they made no effort at all.

We were more disappointed than upset. We simply can't reward bad behavior, although we enjoyed shopping at Ethan Allen for 25 years. There are simply too many competitors who value our business more than it does. Now, all or most of its product is now made in China, and we try to support products made in the U.S.A. At The CareGiver Partnership, we favor brands manufactured here and believe it makes sense to pay a little more for American-made products of higher quality.

"We're sorry that your flight has been cancelled. The good news is, you won't be charged extra for a change to your itinerary and you get one free use of the lavatory."

Chapter 8

Grounded by the Airlines

AH, United Airlines. This is an example of a trip, well conceived and planned and booked seven months in advance, that becomes a disaster due to poor planning by the airline. Again, we present the situation and provide you with an example of how to get your money's worth.

To summarize, on July 7, 2003, we booked two first-class, round-trip tickets, using miles, from Appleton, Wisconsin, to Maui. On the appointed morning in February 2004, during the first leg of our flight, United dropped the ball and didn't have a plane available to take us to Chicago for our connection to Maui. This almost resulted in us arriving a day later. Lynn is claustrophobic, so we decided since it was a long flight, we'd use our miles fly first-class where there is more room. Not only were we not able to sit in first class, we were put in the last row of coach, in the middle seat.

Following is the background of what occurred. You will see that our letter to United's CEO clearly states upfront the compensation we requested, and provides a detailed presentation in a factual manner.

Feb. 27, 2004

Mr. Glenn F. T.
Chairman, President and CEO
UAL Corp.
P.O. Box 66100
Chicago, IL 60666

Subject: Ticket # 0162197390474-75: 2/13/04 from ATW-OGG; 2/23/04 from OGG to ATW

Dear Mr. T.:

The purpose of this letter is to request:

- Two complimentary round-trip, first-class tickets anywhere United flies in the continental United States.

- Reinstatement of at least 30,000 miles to our frequent flyer account (Mileage Plus # XXXX). These miles were debited from our account on July 7, 2003, when we booked the subject transportation directly through United.

- Reimbursement of $85.35 for the most basic of clothing due to our luggage arriving more than 18 hours late. Receipt attached.

- Reimbursement of $164.22 representing the difference between the round-trip fare we paid ($832.12) in order to upgrade to first-class and the regular coach fare posted on your Web site as of Feb. 19 (from ATW to OGG, $667.90).

We are making this request due to the mistakes United made. We booked the trip directly with United on July 7, 2003, a full seven months in advance.

Background

At 5:30 a.m. on Friday, Feb. 13, we received a confirmation from United on our cell phone that our flight UA 5729 from ATW to ORD was on time. Based on this confirmation, we arrived at the airport at 7:15 a.m. to check in. Upon check-in for our flight, we were asked for upgrade vouchers to first class. We told your agent United hadn't sent us vouchers. Your agent called another United representative on the phone and was told that someone at United had made an error on our ticketing. She worked with the person on the phone for some time and was able to correct this mistake.

Next we learned that United, unbeknownst to us, had changed our seating and we would no longer be sitting together on our flight from Chicago to Los Angeles, UA 109.

Third, due to improperly planned maintenance, UAL 5729 (Appleton, Wisconsin, to Chicago, Illinois) was delayed from the 8:22 scheduled departure to 9:45 a.m., even though you had confirmed that the flight was on time and then reconfirmed it again via voice mail that it would depart only 18 minutes late, at 8:40 a.m. Your confirmation system is of little value. Had we known in the morning, when you knew you were experiencing issues, we could have made other arrangements via the Green Bay airport or here in Appleton, Wisconsin (ATW), via Northwest.

According to your people, equipment for flight 5729 wasn't available due to improperly planned maintenance. We were told the delay was United's fault, that a new antenna was installed on the underside of the plane and the maintenance team didn't plan sufficient time during the night for the sealant to properly cure.

Driven by what appears to be an objective of maximizing profit, the announcement of the schedule changes was delayed until the last possible moment in order to keep as many passengers engaged with United. As a result, my wife, Lynn, and I were forced to change to American Airlines, at the request of United, and were not allowed to remain in first class. This is another example of your profit-maximization objective vs. a focus on customer service.

Due to flight UA 5729 (Appleton to Chicago) being further delayed from 9:00 to 9:45 a.m., we were not physically able to make it from Terminal 1 to Terminal 3 at Chicago to connect with the American flight that United booked us on. Our next step was to rebook as standby passengers on American, departing Chicago to Honolulu at 11:15 a.m. We waited approximately 45 minutes at the American gate, only to find there weren't any seats available for us on that flight.

At this point, our cell phone received another message from United, telling us we had been automatically rebooked on a flight the next day, Feb. 14, and would arrive at 7:55 p.m., a full 28 hours after our originally scheduled arrival time. There was no mention made of overnight hotel accommodations in Chicago. We weren't aware who made these arrangements either. Regardless, we had guaranteed reservations in Hawaii that required a 72-hour advance cancellation, at a cost of more than $400 per night.

Following this, we were told by American that it had no flights available to Maui that day, Feb. 13, and we should go back to United. Once again, we ran clear across O'Hare from the last gate in K19 in Terminal 3 back to Terminal 1, United ticketing. At this point, my wife was crying.

At the United ticket counter in Chicago, we approached your service director, Charlotte, who immediately took action, booked us on UA 147 (Chicago to San Francisco) and UA 35 (San Francisco to Maui), and personally walked us to the front of the security line so we could make it to the gate on time. She is to be commended. In all our 30 years of flying, she is the perfect example of delivering customer delight. Smart, well trained and decisive. We are writing her a separate letter to thank her. I would suggest you also recognize her.

Unfortunately, not only were we not able to sit in first class, there were no seats in econo plus. Moreover, we had to sit in the center and window seat on both flights (Chicago to San Francisco and San Francisco to Maui). On the Chicago to San Francisco flight, we had to sit in the last row, where the seats don't recline. As previously mentioned, Lynn suffers from claustrophobia and has occasional panic attacks, which is why the first-

"Excellent service is remembered long after a low price is forgotten."

class upgrade was important to us. Furthermore, we weren't even offered a complimentary drink or meal coupon for our troubles.

The final setback occurred when our luggage didn't arrive with the flight, which reached the gate at 8 p.m., Maui time. After filling out your form in Maui, we didn't receive our luggage until 2:00 the following afternoon. Because we didn't have any other clothes with us, we had to purchase some for the day. This included inexpensive flip-flops, shorts and T-shirts at an inexpensive ABC Store, vs. the resort store we were staying at. The cost for this was $85.35, for which we expect reimbursement (receipt enclosed). Obviously, the start of our 25th wedding anniversary celebration was ruined.

We find it interesting that should we make any change to our schedule whatsoever, you expect us to pay you $100. However, when you change our airline, our seating, our seating class, departure and arrival time, and deliver our luggage late, you feel it's acceptable to offer us nothing, not even a complimentary drink or meal.

It is for this reason that we are making the requests listed in the opening paragraph of this letter.

P.S.

On Saturday, Feb. 21, at 9:30 p.m., we phoned your reservation system to confirm our return trip. We talked to someone named Michele, and she at first said your system showed that we had only *requested* a first-class upgrade. I told her United had confirmed the upgrade with us on July 7, 2003, seven months earlier. After further reviewing our records, she was able to confirm our seat assignments on UA 42 (Maui to Los Angeles) as 4AB and UA 124 (Los Angeles to Chicago O'Hare) as 2HJ.

We asked Michele a question that she couldn't answer, and she gave me your customer service number, 800-877-1327. We called and received a message that it was closed until Monday. We found it remarkable that as an airline that has customers using its services 24/7/365, you don't feel that it is important to have someone available to answer questions. Moreover, your agent Michele failed to tell us that customer service was only a five-day operation. Once again, from a 30-year loyal customer's perspective, this was the third example on one leg of one trip where profit superseded customer service. My wife called your customer service number first thing Monday morning Feb. 23 to confirm our flight and received a recorded message that told her that due to heavy call volume, she should call back later, then the phone disconnected. She tried repeatedly, but to no avail.

On our return flight, Feb. 23, your flight 124 from Los Angeles to Chicago O'Hare, departing at 11:25 p.m., was put on an indefinite delay at 10:30 p.m. Even though UA 126 was scheduled to depart to O'Hare at 11:59, the gate agent refused to allow passengers to book a seat on this flight. Frustrated, I called United reservations and they advised me to go to the gate 70A, where UA 126 was scheduled to depart. I found out there was in fact a number of seats available. Since our luggage wouldn't be transferred, we decided to remain on UA 124, which ultimately departed about 90 minutes late from Los Angeles to O'Hare.

One final comment: No one, I mean no one, ever said, "We're sorry for your inconvenience." From our perspective, United has taken the "customer" out of "customer service." You should focus your investment on your product/service, rather than spending it on image management.

Regards,
Tom Wilson

Tom had to send the following letter to the CEO, because after well over a month, he hadn't yet received a response.

April 9, 2004

Mr. Glenn F. T.
Chairman, President and CEO
UAL Corp.
P.O. Box 66100
Chicago, IL 60666

Subject: Our letter to you dated Feb. 27

Dear Mr. T.:

The purpose of this is to follow up on a letter I mailed to you Feb. 27. On March 8, I did receive a confirmation from Kathy P. in Customer Relations that you had received the letter and a response would be forthcoming shortly. As it has now been a month since she wrote to me, I thought I should follow up with you. I believe a month is a reasonable amount of time, don't you? Perhaps Ms. P.'s response will cross this letter in the mail.

This is another example of the lack of importance that UAL places on customer service.

Regards,
Tom Wilson

As Tom explained in the letter to United's CEO, we were helped by one of the company's gate agents, who provided outstanding customer service. We sent this letter to her to recognize her efforts. It is self-explanatory.

We think it is important to recognize outstanding customer service, because it helps motivate those employees and sets an example for others.

March 14, 2004

United Airlines
Service Director, O'Hare Airport
P.O. Box 66100
Chicago, IL 60666

Dear Charlotte:

The purpose of this letter is to thank you for your help assisting my wife and I at O'Hare on Feb. 13, when we encountered a set of circumstances, the likes of which we've never been confronted in our 30 years of traveling around the world, while traveling from Appleton, Wisconsin, (ATW) to Maui (OGG).

First, let me apologize for the time it has taken me to recognize you for your assistance. I will spare you the gory details of what happened to us; those we've passed on to your CEO. I did want to share with you one paragraph from the letter we mailed to him on Feb. 27:

At the United ticket counter in Chicago, we approached your service director, Charlotte, who immediately took action, booked us on UA 147 (ORD to SFO) and UA 35 (SFO to OGG Maui), and personally walked us to the front of the security line so we could make it to the gate on time. She is to be commended. In all our 30 years of flying, she is the perfect example of delivering customer delight. Smart, well trained and decisive. We are writing her a separate letter to thank her. I would suggest you also recognize her.

Charlotte, United is lucky to have you work on their business. It is rare to find someone as helpful as you were with us on our fateful day trying to make it to Maui. Thank you again for your outstanding assistance.

Best regards,
Tom Wilson
C: Mr. Glenn F. T., chairman, president and CEO, UAL Corp.

We received $85.35 as a reimbursement for the clothing we purchased. It took 63 days from the time we wrote the letter to have this resolved, and it required a follow-up letter to the CEO. We also received two $150 discount coupons for the purchase of two *future* tickets and two $100 vouchers off the purchase of a *future* ticket. This is bad policy. United should provide a refund at some level to say "we're sorry" in addition to discounts on future travel.

United reinstated our 30,000 frequent flyer miles because we were bumped out of first class. They refused, however, to refund the difference we paid for higher-priced tickets in order to upgrade to first class. This was an incremental cost to us of $164.22; I imagine they felt the vouchers were in lieu of this.

So, how did the company do? First, it provided unacceptable service, which was fully in its control because it didn't properly schedule routine maintenance from the Appleton airport. Its gate agent in Chicago provided outstanding customer service and really helped us. Although it was late in responding to our letter to the CEO, it ultimately did respond, apologized and provided a reasonable level of compensation — good, but not great — for the aggravation and disappointment the company caused.

We found it interesting that if an issue arises that results in a customer service issue *and* a baggage issue, United divides the responses. One came from Customer Relations; the other from a baggage claim representative. Since neither copied the other, that we could tell, no one really knew if the issues had been fully resolved. Again, this is a bad practice. A traveler's "bill of rights" is sorely needed.

Delta/Comair

Delta/Comair was Tom's worst travel nightmare in 32 years of traveling. Just before Christmas 2004, he had to fly from Appleton to Cincinnati for business. It was to be a simple trip: a one-hour flight over, two nights in Cincinnati and a one-hour flight home. He started on Monday morning, Dec. 20, at 8:30 a.m. and was to arrive at noon in Cincinnati, Eastern Time. Due to mechanical issues by Comair, the flight was cancelled. He was rerouted on different airlines and arrived six hours late.

On the return trip on Dec. 22, Tom and a business associate were dropped off at the Cincinnati airport for the one-hour flight home on Delta's Comair. They arrived at 4 p.m. for 7 p.m. and 9 p.m. flights. It was freezing rain outside and Delta's Comair planes required deicing. The airport operations worsened with the weather and holiday traffic, and finally at 10 p.m., Comair cancelled all its flights.

The best they could do was book a flight the next night for 9 p.m. They considered renting an SUV and driving home, which would take 10 hours in good weather, but there were no rental cars left. The next plan was to take a cab back to the hotel. The cab line outside already had a 90-minute wait and the weather was getting worse by the minute. They signed up for an airport shuttle and finally made it back to the hotel in downtown Cincinnati at 12:15 a.m.

The next morning Tom learned that Delta/Comair had run out of deicing fluid and that none could be delivered because the interstate was closed due to the weather.

Since it was obvious no planes would be flying and the buses were grounded — the Greyhound drivers were stuck at the hotel, along with the Delta pilots — Tom decided to charter a plane from Appleton to come get them, with instructions to fly into an airport used by Procter & Gamble executives in Cincinnati. The main Cincinnati airport is actually across the river in Kentucky.

Since the weather had cleared, no deicing fluid was required and they made it home in two and a half hours — longer than usual, but they were on a twin-prop four-seater plane. In the end, we learned Comair did not fly to Appleton for another six days. Had Tom not been proactive, he would have spent Christmas at a hotel in Cincinnati.

After the holidays, Tom phoned Delta to request a refund for the round trip. It took three calls and almost three hours of waiting on hold before finally breaking though. Delta offered to provide him with a travel voucher, but he insisted that due to their gross negligence, he wanted the cost of the trip credited back to our credit card. They finally relented and Tom waited a reasonable period of time for the company to follow up on its promise. We noticed the credit card hadn't been credited and called again, going through another 45 minutes of waiting on hold before reaching a person. In the end, we got our credit.

Tom sent Delta's CEO a letter, explaining that his company's gross negligence resulted in significant incremental expenses on his part. Following is the letter:

Dec. 24, 2004

Mr. Gerald G.
Chief Executive Officer
Delta Airlines
Hartsfield Atlanta International Airport
1030 Delta Blvd.
Atlanta, GA 30320-6001

Dear Mr. G.:

The purpose of this letter is to request reimbursement for incremental expenses I incurred due to gross negligence by Delta.

Background

On December 22, 2004, I had a scheduled flight from Covington (Cincinnati airport) to Appleton, Wisconsin, at 9 p.m. on flight 5576 (Comair). Our confirmation number was 3EEMKA.

Due to the gross negligence by Delta (specifics follow), this flight was cancelled on Dec. 22, 23, Christmas Eve, Christmas Day and Dec. 26. Your Rich C., SVP of customer service, blamed the "delays" on the weather (see the article below from your Web site as of Dec. 24).

To add insult to injury, your PR department drafted the following subhead to the release: "Delta assisting customers to change itineraries without charge." It is inconceivable that Delta would even infer they would expect consumers to pay them to change tickets due to negligence on Delta's and Comair's part.

You will also notice the convenient exclusion of any mention of Delta's negligence of not ensuring sufficient supplies of type 3 glycol (deicer). This occurred even though there was more than sufficient warning that a major storm was approaching. It is not relevant that the storm may have consumed abnormal levels of glycol. The fact is that Delta management did not take the necessary steps to ensure sufficient inventory. I obtained this information from several senior Delta pilots who were staying at the same hotel in Cincinnati. They were as upset as we were at the total negligence in planning by Delta.

In addition to this glycol mismanagement, which led to a state of emergency being declared at the Covington (Cincinnati) airport, Delta's computer system for its wholly owned subsidiary, Comair, which was neither properly maintained nor staffed, collapsed, causing all flights to be cancelled. This further exacerbated the situation. Short staffing led to minimal communication. Consumers at Covington were quoted on national TV saying, "The Comair people just didn't seem to care."

I am a frequent traveler and have been traveling worldwide for 30 years. I was a senior executive at Kimberly-Clark when K-C owned Midwest Express. I have yet to witness such a total meltdown in operations. You did not have sufficient glycol, ticket or gate representatives, or representatives to help consumers who attempted to call for direction and help — this in the middle of a winter storm you knew was approaching during the Christmas holiday.

Further, your reservation system was not properly maintained or staffed. I can tell you firsthand there was virtually no communication from your agents, probably because they weren't provided with updates. This was also confirmed by several of your senior pilots. I will also tell you that I attempted to contact Delta on numerous occasions via telephone to determine what I should do. During these calls, I waited an hour each time before disconnecting; there was never an option to leave a message for a return call. I was finally able to reach someone during the evening on Christmas Eve, again after being on hold for 30+ minutes.

To add further insult to injury, your spokeswoman Tanya D. (Atlanta) was quoted on Dec. 24 in the Cincinnati Enquirer as being "unaware of the situation" at the Cincinnati airport. The airport had been declared a crisis by the government due to Delta's lack of planning, requiring the National Guard to be called in. Your spokesperson, by her own admission, was totally unaware of what was going on.

You should also know that the first leg of our trip, which occurred on Monday, Dec. 20, from Appleton to Cincinnati on Flight 5054 was cancelled. As a result of having to reroute on different airlines through different airports, we arrived in Cincinnati six hours late.

Next Steps

As a consequence of Delta's gross negligence (glycol, reservation systems and staffing), I am seeking reimbursement for incremental hotel and carriage costs (from the Cincinnati airport to downtown Cincinnati) and return transportation to Appleton from Cincinnati.

The total incremental cost for myself and a business associate is $2,152.66. Following are details of our out-of-pocket expenses:

- Shuttle from Cincinnati airport to downtown via Airport Executive, Inc. the night of Dec. 22, after Delta/Comair cancelled the original flight: $50.

- Two rooms at the Millennium Hotel for myself and a business associate during the night of Dec. 22: $232.66.

- Cab from Millennium to Lunken Field, Ohio, on Dec. 23: $20.

- Charter flight from Lunken Field to Appleton on Dec. 23; charter was with MaxAir (Appleton) on a four-person, twin-engine Barrow (tail # N6025Y): $1,830.

Your check in the amount of $2,152.66 should be made out to me and mailed to the address below. Full documentation of expenses will be provided upon request.

In summary, I am a long-time Delta customer who is merely seeking reimbursement for justified out-of-pocket expenses caused by negligence on Delta's part.

If I am not reimbursed for these expenses, I will choose any other airline over Delta for all future travel for myself and our employees.

Please let me know if you have any questions.

Regards,
Tom Wilson

On Jan. 19, Tom received a letter from a person in Delta's "Customer Care" who said the company would need to decline our request for a refund of our travel costs. It did, however, agree to reimburse him for $302.66, 14 percent of the actual out-of-pocket costs. At least we were now only out $1,850. It also graciously credited our frequent flyer account with 25,000 miles. The letter was well written and apologetic.

To demonstrate how serious this issue was, a Wall Street Journal article on Jan. 18, 2005, announced that the president of Delta's Comair unit was leaving to pursue other opportunities. This is generally corporate code for "was fired." We were proud of Delta's management; the company took a stance and set a tone for the organization that poor customer service wouldn't be tolerated.

Tom recalled thinking, while stranded in Cincinnati and watching the news during the meltdown, that if he were president of Comair, he would have been front and center at the airport, visible to the team and managing media relations as best as he could. Instead the company allowed a spokeswoman in Delta's Atlanta office to release a statement where she was quoted as being "unaware of the situation" at the airport, even though it had been declared in a state of crisis and the National Guard had been called in.

In the end, Delta did offset a portion of our incremental cost. It completely refunded the round-trip ticket, paid for all the incremental expenses for an additional night and day in Cincinnati, excluding the cost of the charter flight, and added 25,000 miles to our Delta frequent flyer account. It responded to our correspondence in a timely manner — 24 days — with an apologetic and well-written letter that told us the company had read and fully comprehended Tom's letter to the CEO.

We almost certainly received more from Delta than 99 percent of the customers who were unfortunate to get stuck in the pre-Christmas meltdown. The reason we did was due to the following factors:

- We communicated with the company immediately following the event, both on the phone and in writing. We knew they were in a state of crisis and management probably allowed more decision-making at lower levels to quickly resolve issues. This was not a situation where it could waste time operating under the normally stifling chain-of-command decision-making process.

- We put our request in writing and were specific in what we were asking for.

- We knew that if the airlines can point to weather as the cause of problems, they are off the hook and don't have to compensate you. We also knew from our conversations with Delta's pilots that the core issue was poor planning (no deicing fluid) and poor systems (reservation system crash). This is where we placed the blame. The company knew it was the cause and couldn't deny it.

The saddest part were the young families traveling with infants who didn't know what to do in a situation like this. Tom saw the looks on their faces, confused and frustrated with no one to turn to for answers. Many ultimately spent Christmas in the airport or at a local motel that they perhaps couldn't afford. We couldn't help but think how the president of Comair and his boss were enjoying Christmas with their families. It was a disgrace.

"If you do build a great experience, customers tell each other about that.
Word of mouth is very powerful."

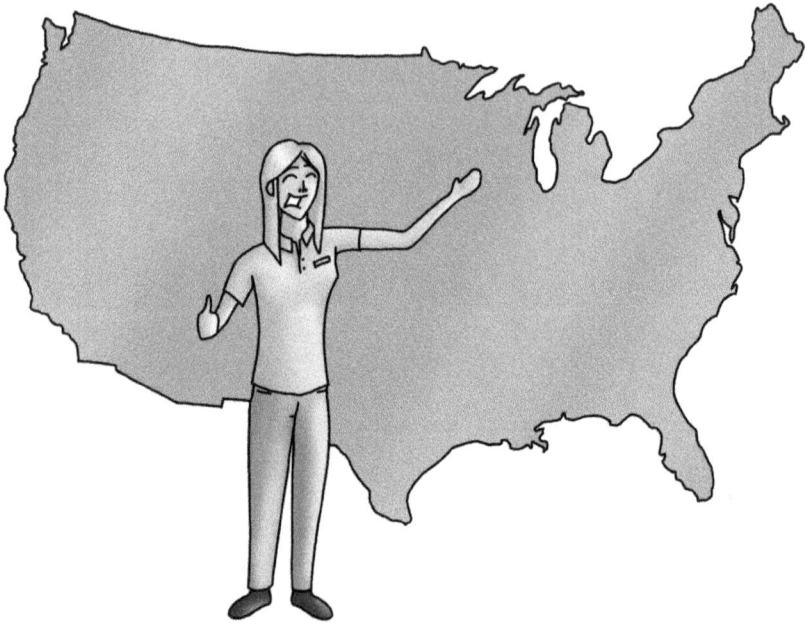

"Our map says you have coverage. So you have coverage. The map is never wrong. That's our policy. Oh, and the all-inclusive plan is now limited."

Chapter 9

Dropped by the Wireless Companies

SINCE wireless began its exponential growth curve, our experience — along with most consumers', it seems — with a number of companies has been nothing but disappointing. If memory serves correct, we have been with five carriers: Cellulink, PrimeCo, Alltel, Sprint and AT&T. With all the mergers, acquisitions, name changes and new names, you may not recognize PrimeCo and Alltel. Alltel is on at least its third name change that we're aware of.

We don't have statistics on consumer satisfaction with the carriers, but I suspect it is poor, from what we've observed and the conversations we've had with family, friends and business associates. We previously discussed the concept of the Net Promoter Score, or NPS. We suspect all the major cell phone companies have a negative NPS, meaning more customers dislike the service than are enjoying it. This would certainly be true for AT&T customers in major cities who experience problems with their service.

Our first cellular example occurred when advertising claims from an organization named PrimeCo lured us to them for better service. It didn't take long before we realized how poor it was. As a "newbie" to cellular service, we didn't understand the phone was proprietary to the company's system.

Before Aug. 18, 1998

Mr. Lowell M.
Chief Executive Officer
PrimeCo Personal Communications, L.P.
6 Campus Circle
Westlake, TX 76262

Dear Mr. M.:

The purpose of this e-mail is to provide you with feedback regarding your customer service.

Several months ago, we purchased a Qualcomm phone from Circuit City and switched from Cellulink (analog phone) to PrimeCo. We could have purchased a digital phone from Cellulink; however, we were led to believe PrimeCo was better.

We have found that PrimeCo service does not meet our needs, because the digital signal area is very limited and PrimeCo does not have any Prime Travel cities in our area (Appleton, Wisconsin) that provide seamless analog calls. This was verified by Charla, one of your representatives.

I talked to Karen at your Appleton store and told her our dilemma. She mentioned you are working on expanding coverage, but didn't know when it might be available. Since the coverage does not at all meet our needs, we need to discontinue service. However, since we recently paid about $150 for our phone, we took it to Cellulink to have it converted to its analog service.

They attempted to set up the phone using the most common six-digit security codes (654321, 111111 and 000000). This didn't work. We called PrimeCo to obtain the code and were told there was a $200+ charge.

We went through three levels of your customer care and were told we have no choice. It would cost us $200+ to "purchase" the code from

PrimeCo, even though we own the phone and signed no agreement relating to a security code.

We were on the phone for more than an hour, until Charla asked if she could have a customer care supervisor call us back in 10 minutes. We waited for almost an hour for Sue from your Tampa office to call us back. She told us the same thing the other two people we talked with did — that we could buy the security code from PrimeCo for $200+ for a phone that we paid about $150 for.

As we have experienced your gauntlet of customer care representatives, which were all courteous, and we have limited time, we are writing directly to you. We expect you to talk with your people and immediately authorize one of two actions:

1) E-mail our code to _____.

2) Reimburse us for the cost of our phone.

If we were leading a business, we would be incensed if we found any one of our team treating customers the way we have been treated.

Lowell, let us share something with you as you consider which action to take: A study conducted by Technical Assistance Research Programs, Inc., which was commissioned by the U.S. Department of Consumer Affairs, found 96 percent of PrimeCo consumers won't let you know they are dissatisfied; of these, up to 90 percent won't buy again from PrimeCo or will discontinue service; you can win back up to 70 percent of customers with a complaint by resolving the problem; and if you handle problems quickly and well, 95 percent will become loyal customers.

Sincerely,
Thomas E. Wilson
Account # 0000000000-0

Sept. 4, 1998

Mr. Lowell M.
Chief Executive Officer
PrimeCo Personal Communications, L.P.
6 Campus Circle
Westlake, TX 76262

Mr. M.:

Your customer care representative, Sue, successfully solved our problem, as noted below in the previous e-mail I sent you, by allowing us to return our phone and accessories for a full refund. We are in the process of waiting for her to send a box so that we may send it back to you via Federal Express. It did, however, take us more than two hours on the phone, talking with four customer care representatives to arrange this.

A final thought we would like to leave with you for consideration deals with your policy of "selling" the six-digit security code. The way it currently works is false and misleading. More importantly, essentially you are forcing customers to stay with you or throw away their phones. We were never told verbally or in writing that should we wish to use the phone with another carrier, we would have to purchase a security code.

We suggest you implement one of the following changes:

- Eliminate the policy altogether (your best choice).

- Have customers sign, in writing, a clear understanding that the only way they will be able to use the phone with another carrier is to pay $200+, more than the price of the phone. This should be communicated before the sale is made by you or by third parties like Circuit City.

I would be interested in knowing which of the two options you choose. Thank you in advance.

(He never responded.)

After Sept. 4, 1998

Mr. Lowell M.
Chief Executive Officer
PrimeCo Personal Communications, L.P.
6 Campus Circle
Westlake, TX 76262

Mr. M.:

The purpose of this letter is to share with you our experience with PrimeCo service in Appleton, Wisconsin. I feel the matter is important enough to write to you, the CEO, directly. And as an officer of a Fortune 200 company, I know I would want to be aware of a situation like this. I know you are busy; so am I. I promise this matter is worth 10 minutes of your time.

I e-mailed Jim G. two times about two weeks ago and asked that the e-mail be forwarded to you. Since I haven't heard anything, I am writing directly to you.

Background

Several months ago, I purchased a Qualcomm phone from Circuit City in Appleton, Wisconsin, and switched from Cellulink to PrimeCo. I could have purchased a digital phone from Cellulink and stayed with them; however, I was led to believe PrimeCo had superior service.

After using the phone and PrimeCo service for several months, I found the service does not meet our needs because the digital signal area is very limited. Moreover, PrimeCo does not have any Prime Travel cities in our area that provide seamless analog/digital calls. Charla, one of your representatives, verified this for me.

I talked to Karen at your Appleton, Wisconsin, kiosk and told her our dilemma. She said PrimeCo was expanding coverage but didn't know when it might be available. Since the coverage did not at all meet our needs, I had to switch back to Cellulink. To accomplish this, I took the phone to Cellulink to have it converted to its analog service.

Cellulink attempted to set up the phone using the most common six-digit security code digits. Since none of these worked, I called PrimeCo to obtain the code and was told there would be an administrative fee. I own the phone and had not received anything verbally or in writing about paying an "administrative" fee of $200 should I switch services.

I went through three levels of your customer care on the phone and a visit to your kiosk and was told that I had no choice but to pay $200+ to purchase the code from PrimeCo.

After being on the phone for more than an hour, Charla asked if she could have a supervisor call me back in 10 minutes. I waited almost an hour before Sue from your Tampa office called me back. Sue told me the same thing, that I could buy the security code from PrimeCo for $200+ for a phone that I paid about $150 for.

After a good deal of dialog, Sue ultimately allowed me to return our phone and accessories for a refund. On Aug. 18, I returned them via Federal Express, in addition to faxing a copy of the original purchase receipt to a number provided by Sue. I have not yet heard anything. Could you please check this for me? In order to get to this point, it took me more than two hours on the phone with your care representatives.

The practice of charging a $200+ administrative fee for the six-digit security code is false and misleading. Moreover, it is just plain bad business. I would like you to implement one of the two following changes:

- Eliminate the practice altogether (your best choice).

- At minimum, have customers sign a clear understanding that the only way they will be able to use the phone with another carrier is to pay $200+ (more than the price of the phone). This should be communicated before PrimeCo, or a third party like Circuit City, make the sale.

Please let me know which of the two options you choose. Thank you in advance.

Sincerely,
Tom Wilson

C:

Bell Atlantic
1095 Avenue of the Americas
New York, NY 10036

Raymond W. Smith
Chairman of the Board and CEO

Ivan G. Seidenberg
Vice chairman, president and COO

Lawrence T. Babbio, Jr.
President and CEO, Network Group
Chairman, Global Wireless Group

James G. Cullen
President and CEO, Telecom Group

Alexander H. Good
Executive VP, Strategy and Corporate Development

Jacquelyn B. Gates
VP, Ethics and Corporate Compliance

James R. Young
Executive VP, General Counsel

Sam Ginn
Chairman of the Board and CEO
AirTouch Communications, Inc.

Rhoda H. Karpatkin
President and CEO, Circuit City
9950 Mayland Drive
Richmond VA 23233

Wisconsin Attorney General
James E. Doyle

It might appear from the above copy list that Tom was in overload mode, but PrimeCo was a combination of a number of organizations, and he thought it important to cover all the bases. He also felt insulted enough with this experience to copy a number of the officers, hoping that one letter might actually reach one and the individual might bring up the subject in a staff meeting.

Unfortunately, as you can see from the correspondence above, it took an enormous effort to get the phone returned and our money back. Even at that point, we had to sign up with another cell phone company.

This is an example that borderlines on fraud, in our view. Our association with PrimeCo was short-lived, and so was the brand. While PrimeCo won some advertising awards, the brand itself died — perhaps due to similar customer service that we experienced.

CenturyTel

This is an example of an organization overpromising and underdelivering — a poor marketing and customer service strategy, and one that will surely ruin the equity of a brand over time. Before providing you with the background, it is helpful to have an understanding of how companies develop claims for their products and services.

In order to develop a winning product or service, a company should deliver against what it promises. Ideally, it delivers more than promised. In the marketing world, it is customary to test a new or improved product or service by exposing consumers to it in focus groups, using a written description that frequently includes visuals. This is called a concept board and may look like a magazine advertisement.

Each word and visual element of the offering is probed in depth. Sometimes, consumers find certain claims or words hard to understand or unbelievable. Through an iterative process using a series of focus groups or triads, the words and pictures are refined. To learn more about this go to www.centerbraininc.com. CenterBrain is a marketing consultancy that works with brands such as Depend, Elmer's, Vise Grip, Visa and Kotex to position new or improved products. It determines the best approach to tell consumers about the product. One of its hallmarks is to determine, for each brand it works with, what it calls the Three T's, which we discussed earlier:

Tangible Benefit: Your brand's selling proposition should quickly answer the consumer's question of, "What's in it for me?"

Truth: Support for the selling proposition is grounded in logic.

That's Me: A universal insight is acknowledged that lets the customer know your brand understands her better than any other.

Typically, at this stage, the concept will be presented to several hundred consumers in order to gain their input on a range of measures. Companies want to know how likely you would be to purchase the product or service after viewing the concept, if you found anything confusing or hard to believe, how you rate the value, how often you might purchase and many other measures. Today, much of this type of research is conducted online.

Marketing research companies maintain lists of tens of thousands of consumers who have agreed to participate in research questionnaires from time to time. The lists may include data on pet ownership, age, income and geographic location, so they can target certain groups of consumers, such as pet owners or households with infants in diapers. At The CareGiver Partnership, we conduct a great deal of research for manufacturers and those providing services to boomers and seniors.

Consumers on the lists receive e-mail with a new survey to complete. They go to the site and are presented with a series of questions. In the case of a quantitative concept study, they're asked to view the concept or mock ad, and following this, are presented with a series of questions about it. The marketing research company collects the data electronically, and then analyzes it.

For example, in the case of disposable diapers, the manufacturer may be interested in how first-time moms responded to a concept for a new or improved diaper compared to moms who have already had a child. The makers of Huggies diapers may want to know how moms who normally purchase Pampers have responded. After the data is collected, it is sliced and diced — technically termed "cross tabbing" — in any number of ways.

Once a company is satisfied that it has developed a concept that successfully presents the new product or service, it conducts another test, one more expensive and complicated, to determine if the product lives up to the claims made in the concept.

The process involves placing product with those consumers who said in the online quantitative concept that they would be likely to purchase it. In the case of disposable diapers, they are shipped to consumers. After a specified period, they are asked to complete a series of questions about the likelihood of purchasing the new or improved diapers. They also are presented with a battery of questions to determine how well it lives up to the claims presented in the concept.

At this point, it's critical that consumers' purchase intent after trying the new diaper is as high, or ideally, higher than it was before they had an opportunity to try it. For example, in the case of disposable diapers, let's say 60 percent of consumers in the study said they would definitely or probably purchase the new, improved diaper after being exposed to the concept only, with no product to try. After consumers try the product, ideally at least 60 percent or more give it the same purchase intent rating. In the case of CenturyTel, we're not sure the company would have seen this occur. We'll explain why.

CenturyTel, now CenturyLink, was known by at least one other name prior to the time we signed up with it. It marketed its services under the brand Alltel, then Center Tel and now CenturyLink. We signed up because the company Tom was working for at the time had a corporate account and employees were offered a 12 percent discount.

As is the case today, the rates, plans, options and coverage areas were confusing. We figured someone at Kimberly-Clark had analyzed the various offerings and determined that CenturyTel offered the best combination of service and price. Of particular importance was the coverage area, because we had two daughters away at college and Tom traveled a great deal. Based on the coverage maps presented to us, and along with other factors, we switched.

The service was not any better than our previous carrier's. It had serious problems, including dropped calls and fuzzy connections, even in our hometown. At this point in our lives, we had three phones, including two for our daughters, and Tom had a CenturyTel phone though work.

We struggled with the service, feeling that while it was lacking, it was probably as good as it got. However, the poor service culminated one day when a serious emergency occurred, and there was a lack of service in an area advertised as a coverage zone, about one mile from an interstate highway.

Our youngest daughter was driving home from college for the weekend on a beautiful fall afternoon. She was attending the University of Wisconsin in Stevens Point. On that particular day, Tom was attending a global marketing conference in Green Lake, Wisconsin, about 50 miles away.

During the afternoon, a person from the conference center entered Tom's meeting room to give him a message that read, "Emergency! Call Julie (his administrative assistant) immediately." Alarmed, he tried calling the office from his work cell phone, but had no service. He located a bank of pay phones to find they were all being used. Finally, when one was free, he called Julie. She said she had received a call from our daughter but could barely make it out. The call lasted about 10 seconds before it was dropped, and it came from within a mile of Interstate Highway 39, an area that was clearly within the advertised calling area.

Julie said that all she could hear through the static was our daughter saying something about her car being on fire. Tom asked her to call him at the conference center if she heard back, then tried calling from his cell phone again, to no avail. Absolutely no service. He even phoned our daughter's cell phone using a landline, but couldn't make a connection.

Before cell phones became a necessity, one of the primary reasons consumers purchased them was for safety in a situation like the one just described. We had been utterly let down at the one time we really needed to depend on CenturyTel's service. In our view, the company had breached our agreement by not providing service as advertised.

We ultimately learned that our daughter had just begun her hour-and-fifteen-minute journey home and had attempted to adjust the outside mirror of her Blazer using the switch, but couldn't get it to work. She decided to quit trying and focus on her driving. Shortly after passing over Interstate 39, about 10 minutes from campus, she smelled something and noticed smoke coming from the door. After pulling over to the side of the road to investigate, she saw the smoke had turned to fire. She attempted to phone for help, but couldn't complete a call. She then tried calling Tom at work, not knowing he was at the conference. His assistant answered the phone and heard her cryptic message for a few seconds.

The fire continued spreading, yet her cell phone wouldn't connect to 911. She flagged down a driver, who was able to place an emergency call for help using his cell phone. I don't know who his carrier was, but it's obvious it wasn't CenturyTel. Lynn picked up our daughter and we ultimately had the vehicle towed an hour back to our hometown for repairs, which totaled more than $3,000.

This emergency situation was the proverbial straw that broke the camel's back. We decided it was time to move to another carrier. Tom contacted the CEO of CenturyTel, indicating we were terminating our service due to a breach of contract. We provided him with the details of what had occurred and offered to return all the equipment without expectation of a refund. This included four phones, multiple chargers, batteries and hands-free kits. Tom received a letter from a customer care representative, saying he was sorry for what had occurred, but he didn't address the subject of returning the equipment. We made the switch to Sprint.

The next contact CenturyTel made with us was an invoice for $600 for terminating our agreement early. Tom wrote back directly to the CEO, informing him we didn't have any intention of making the payment because his company breached the agreement by not providing service as advertised. We made a second offer to return the equipment. To this, Tom received a reply from the same representative, indicating he would be held responsible for the payment. Tom wrote back, copying the CEO once again, stating not only were we not paying this, but if we did not hear back within 30 days, we were donating the equipment. There was no further response on CenturyTel's part so we disposed of it.

The next correspondence was from a collection agency. Tom immediately wrote back to them, informing the agency we had a dispute with the company, copied CenturyTel on the correspondence and suggested the collection agency confer with the CEO. That was the last we heard from them.

The lessons here, from a consumer perspective, are to maintain complete and accurate records of correspondence, names and any follow-up; maintain timely contact; and communicate expectations and what your intentions are in a reasonable, unemotional, nonthreatening manner. We had been long-term, loyal customers and heavy users of CenturyTel's services. In our case, the CEO decided that simply turning us over to a collection agency was his best course of action to build long-term brand equity and drive profitability. He was a pinhead sitting in his ivory tower and could care less about an individual customer. You can imagine how many people we've told this story to. It's not like there aren't other cellular providers.

In this example, our account was turned over to a collection agency. We'd never dealt with this before. Common sense told us the collection agency wasn't going to be highly motivated trying to collect in a case where the company was at fault and after we had tried in vain to resolve the situation directly with the CEO. When dealing with a collection agency, it is important to respond to requests in a timely manner; otherwise, it may affect your credit rating. Don't simply throw away the letters.

Speaking of credit ratings, we subscribe to a service that monitors all requests for our credit history and provides us with reports on our rating.

"In the world of Internet customer service, it's important to remember your competitor is only one mouse click away."

Any time anyone accesses our credit history, we get an e-mail indicating when it occurred, who requested it and why. For example, let's say we go to Best Buy and purchase a television and they offer us a no-payment arrangement for 18 months. We fill out a credit application in the store, are approved on the spot and within a month or so, we get an e-mail saying our credit history had been accessed. We can see exactly who it was — typically a finance company Best Buy has a marketing arrangement with, in this example. We like this service, Equifax, because we can monitor suspicious activity and protect ourselves from identify theft.

The customer service lesson for businesses is the same as we are espousing throughout this book: You don't build brand equity and ultimately profitability by attempting to sell product and services that don't deliver. David Ogilvy, who formed one of the largest advertising agencies in the world, had a saying about this: "The consumer is not stupid. She's your wife."

Don't treat every consumer request the same. Each time a consumer takes the time to contact you about your product or service, you must respond in a way that's appropriate to the situation. In this example, CenturyTel's CEO clearly insulted us when he turned the collection agency on us. In the end, his decision may have cost his organization 10 times the revenue he had already lost due to poor service, simply because of word of mouth. The unfortunate customer care representative's hands were probably tied to a procedure manual that provided him with few options to effectively manage the situation.

What could they have done? First, no company wants to lose a client. It happens; we've dealt with it at The CareGiver Partnership. Step one with us is, if we have done something wrong or let the customer down, we apologize. CenturyTel didn't attempt this. Its strategy should have been to call, apologize and offer to negotiate. They might have said, "We want to thank you for being a great customer (we had four lines, had been with them for years and always paid on time) and are sorry we didn't meet your expectations. Normally, we expect customers to make good on the cancellation penalty if they exit an agreement early. In your case, we would like to offer the following ..."

Its objective should have been to have us leave CenturyTel with a positive perception of the company, in the hopes of regaining our confidence in the future with an improved service offer. What they accomplished was to convince us to never consider doing business with them again in the future and to have us tell others about the lousy way they treated us. Unfortunately, as far as we know, they don't have required classes on customer service in MBA school.

There is a metric in business called "customer lifetime value." Business leaders have to consider the *real* lifetime value — not just the period from when a customer begins buying your product or service and when they discontinue, but the potential to win back the customer for his lifetime. Sending a collection agency after a customer when the company is at fault is poor business strategy. Glen P., the CEO, obviously didn't care enough about customers; after all he was earning more than $1 million per year.

Following is the correspondence with CenturyTel:

March 25, 2002

CenturyTel
Appleton Division
311A Mall Drive
Appleton, WI 54912

Subject: Discontinuation of Service

To Whom It May Concern:

This will serve notice to discontinue service to the following phone numbers upon receipt of this request.

Unfortunately, after being a loyal customer for many years and through many ownership changes, I found the service was not able to deliver connections in the calling area as advertised.

Please let me know if you have any questions. I would like a confirmation that service has been discontinued.

Regards,
Tom Wilson

April 22, 2002

Mr. Glen F. P.
President, CEO
100 CenturyTel Drive
Monroe, LA 71203

Dear Mr. P.:

The purpose of this letter is to make you aware that after being a loyal customer over a number of years, with several phones and a number of ownership changes on your part, I was forced to discontinue service because CenturyTel was not able to deliver service as advertised.

I found on a number of occasions that our family could not make connections within our calling area. This included calls to Appleton from Green Lake and Madison, Wisconsin. The most distressing example was when our daughter's car caught on fire due to an electrical short, and contact could not be made to or from Stevens Point within a mile of an interstate.

I mentioned this to your people in the Appleton store on several occasions and was told that I "should" have been able to make a call. *(There's that "should" word again; see The Four Bad Words.)* Moreover, most of our connections were consistently poor. Regardless, I held on (and actually added phones), hoping that with more towers and upgraded service, things would improve. It didn't for me.

I was forced to discontinue service with CenturyTel. I had no choice, as CenturyTel was not delivering on its service promise and, therefore, there was a breach of contract.

To add insult to injury to a long-time, loyal and faithful customer, I received a final invoice that included $600 in cancellation charges. I do not intend to pay those charges because CenturyTel breached its contract with me. I am, however, enclosing payment of $29.48 to cover the remaining balance of our obligation.

We are willing to return our equipment, but will donate it to Goodwill if we don't hear from you.

Best regards,
Tom Wilson

May 17, 2002

CenturyTel
P.O. Box 6002
Marion, LA 71260-6002

To Whom It May Concern:

I have been communicating with Glen F. P. about these penalty charges. I informed him that:

- I was a loyal customer for many years.

- I was a heavy-user customer, having purchased at least five phones, accessories and four hands-free kits.

- CenturyTel did not provide service as advertised. On one occasion, during an emergency, calls could not be made from two areas within the calling area, not related to defective phones. I could no longer rely on the system.

- I do not intend to pay the $600 cancellation fee. CenturyTel breached its contract by not providing service as advertised.

- I have agreed to return the equipment. Including the hands-free kits, without expectation of payment.

I was forced to discontinue our service with CenturyTel. I had no choice, as CenturyTel was not delivering on its service promise.

Please let me know if you would like the equipment returned.

Sincerely,
Tom Wilson

May 23, 2002

Mr. Trey A.
Quality Assurance Representative
CenturyTel
P.O. Box 4065
Monroe, LA 71211-4065

Dear Mr. A.:

This responds to your letter dated May 17. Since you did not respond to the offer I made to return the equipment, please be advised that I plan to dispose of it within 30 days if I do not hear from you.

Also, to reiterate, I do not plan to pay the termination fees. As previously mentioned, CenturyTel failed to provide adequate service as advertised. The fact that CenturyTel does not have records of conversations with me is not our concern nor within our control.

You should know that after three contacts in writing with CenturyTel, including two to your CEO, no one from CenturyTel has made any effort to contact me. I think this a clear and specific example of your organization's lack of concern for customer service.

I must say that I am very surprised at CenturyTel's position, given that I was a long-term customer and a heavy user who consistently made prompt payments.

Regards,
Tom Wilson

June 19, 2002

CenturyTel
P.O. Box 6002
Marion, LA 71260-6002

To Whom It May Concern:

Please be advised that I do not intend to pay the $600 early cancellation penalty on the enclosed invoice.

CenturyTel did not provide service as advertised. On one occasion, during an emergency, calls could not be made from two locations within the advertised service area, not related to defective phones. I could no longer rely on your system. CenturyTel breached the contract by not providing service as advertised.

I have agreed to return the equipment, including the hands-free kits.

I was forced to discontinue our service with CenturyTel. I had no choice, as CenturyTel was not delivering on its service promise.

Tom Wilson

July 11, 2002

Mr. Glen F. P.
President and CEO
CenturyTel
100 CenturyTel Drive
Monroe, LA 71203

Mr. Trey A.
Quality Assurance Representative
CenturyTel
P.O. Box 4065
Monroe, LA 71211-4065

Dear Messrs P. and A.:

The purpose of this letter is to let you know I will dispose of the CenturyTel Nokia phones and hands-free kits, since I did not hear back from you or Mr. A. following a May 22 letter.

I thought I would also give you further feedback regarding customer service at CenturyTel. As I mentioned, after three contacts in writing with CenturyTel, including letters to yourself and Mr. A., no one from CenturyTel made any effort to contact me regarding the specific service issues I experienced. Again, this is a clear and specific example of your organization's lack of concern for its customers.

Yesterday, July 10, Jennifer from your company phoned and left a message asking that I call her. I promptly returned her phone call as soon as I got home from work at about 5:30 p.m. After being forced to push buttons and make choices, I then waited on hold for 22 minutes. I reached a representative whose name was also Jennifer and told her I was returning the other Jennifer's call. She asked for our account information and I informed her I was no longer a customer. She then asked for a Social Security number, which I provided to her.

She couldn't locate any information relating to that number or our account, or the reason Jennifer phoned. *(Note: This is an example of not having the right tools.)* She asked me what Jennifer wanted and I told her I didn't know since she hadn't left a message. I requested that if the other Jennifer phoned again, that she leave a direct phone number because I didn't want to have to wait on hold again.

I thought this constructive criticism might be helpful.

Regards,
Tom Wilson

Sprint

Sprint presented us with three customer service examples to share, one dealing with its billing system and two concerning its marketing practices.

From a marketing purist perspective, we think Sprint has done a good job building its brand, that is until it merged with Nextel. It had a consistent look and feel in its advertising, Web site, printed material and retail locations, down to the outfits its associates wear. The company then merged with Nextel and had different colors, a conglomeration of names and two incompatible systems. There was nothing really in it for the consumer, as far as we could tell.

We do think Sprint makes it very challenging to do business with. In fact, we've gotten to the point where we've totally lost confidence in its systems. Its employees, however, have been reasonably empowered to work around the system's shortfalls.

Sprint is trying to operate a mostly robotic company. Its massive layoffs have been well publicized. In a drive for improved efficiencies, it appears to be replacing people with systems. We're not sure where the customer fits into this model. If you call, you get to listen to a digital woman route you through a state-of-the-art voice command system.

During our time with Sprint, we've had to scrutinize our bill each month because of errors — not something we look forward to. We had five lines by this point and make a great deal of calls, so examining the bill is time consuming, not to mention challenging to decipher. During March 2008, Sprint "upgraded" its invoicing. At that point, we noticed new charges, such as "casual data usage" and "equipment protection."

In 2004, Tom left a job where he had a Sprint cell phone. He wanted to keep his phone number, which required having his employer send Sprint an authorization. It all happened in one day — simple! At the same time, he went to our local Sprint store to add a new phone to our account, along with the other four, making Tom's the new master phone number. We also wanted to increase our minutes because we were forming a new business.

Our bill should have been in the $150 range. We received a bill for $373.03. Tom had to go to the store and explain the bill to the store manager, who credited our account $228.47. We couldn't do this over the phone; Tom had to make a special trip to the store.

At the beginning of the next billing cycle, we went to the store to ensure the changes had been properly made, at the request of the store manager! The changes were confirmed and a few days later, we received our bill for the next period, totaling $916.23, including a balance of $144.56 from the previous month. We were charged $771.67 for the previous billing cycle, when our bill should have been $168. After we e-mailed the store manager, he credited our account $603.67. He handled it in a professional, courteous and timely manner. He obviously had good training, people skills and was empowered. But we had to make several phone calls, two trips to the store and a couple of e-mails to clear this up.

Doing business with Sprint scared us. Its systems simply weren't working. I think the examples we provided are clear evidence. For example, if you wanted to change our plan, we had to physically visit the store the first day of our billing cycle. They didn't have the capability to make the change in the system, which is very strange for a company that boasted about its technological advancements.

We also had issues with the purchase of two phones. The first was to offer a $130 rebate. The second, purchased in April, was to have a $150 rebate. On both occasions, the rebates were incorrectly denied.

In early January 2004, our daughter purchased a new phone from Sprint because her previous one quit working. She was enticed to purchase a certain model by the sales representative because of the $130 rebate, and she immediately sent in the rebate form and appropriate attachments. Sprint claims a rebate check takes eight to 14 weeks to process. After sending it in and waiting, our daughter received a postcard saying she didn't qualify for the rebate. She then called several times but couldn't get through.

In late April, Tom made a trip to the Sprint store and told a customer service representative she had been denied. The rep looked up her purchase record and told Tom she "should" have qualified. Of course, they couldn't take care of this at the store, as they don't "do" rebates.

Tom phoned our daughter at college and told her what he discovered. She called Sprint and was forced to push buttons, make choices and wait on hold for 20 minutes. She explained her situation to another customer service representative, who told her Sprint was experiencing problems and that she did in fact qualify. One would expect an apology and an attempt to rush a check when a customer had to wait due to an admitted error on the company's part. Not Sprint. The rebate check ultimately arrived just shy of five months after purchasing the phone. It took less time to conclude some major operations in the Iraq war. Why does it take an all-digital company up to 14 weeks to mail a customer a check, especially after it made the mistake?

At The CareGiver Partnership, if there is an error on our part, we immediately apologize and discount the customer's current order. This is true even if a customer tells us she had a problem figuring out how to place an order on our Web site. We assume it's our fault because we should have made it more intuitive, and for that, we discount the order. This leads us to a key point: Customers realize problems will occur, so if you do cause an issue with a customer, it's how you deal with it that makes the difference.

Did we learn from this situation? We did, but had no choice and needed another new phone. We couldn't switch carriers because we had five phones on a plan with 4,500 minutes. We were locked in, just where the cell phone companies want you. The phone Tom was interested in had a $150 rebate. It was advertised online, but wasn't available in the stores or for purchase online — the customer had to call to get it, which didn't make much sense.

As soon as our new phone arrived, Tom began the process of preparing to send in for the rebate. First, the product didn't ship with an invoice, only a packing slip, and a sales slip was required for a rebate. Then there's the waiting period of up to 14 weeks. After waiting for a number of weeks, Tom also received a postcard saying he didn't qualify because he had a business account, which wasn't true.

We have to give credit to Sprint in one area, however: Tom ordered the phone in the afternoon, it arrived the next afternoon via FedEx and there was no extra shipping charge. The company exceeded our expectations in this regard. But why does it take so long to process a rebate? Perhaps it should have the U.S. government process its rebates; the government can get tax refund checks out more quickly than that. The reason is that Sprint really didn't take customer service seriously. Maybe it was outsourcing rebate processing to an outside vendor who offered cost savings if it could take its time processing the paperwork. Again, who is looking out for you?

Following is the letter Tom enclosed with the rebate paperwork and packing slips.

May 2004

To Whom It May Concern:

Enclosed is our packing slip from the Sanyo PM-8200 phone I purchased directly from you. I did not receive a sales receipt in the carton you sent me, only this packing slip as proof of purchase. The order number was PN50098001 and it was ordered on April 26, 2004. Please send our $150 rebate to the address below.

Regards,
Tom Wilson

In early June, Tom received a postcard telling him the request for the rebate was denied. Once again, he had to call Sprint, push buttons, make choices and wait on hold. He finally had an opportunity to explain our situation to a rep who looked up our account, said there had been a mistake and she would process the rebate. She didn't apologize. She didn't say she'd expedite our rebate or credit our account $150. She just said she'd process it.

After experiencing two back-to-back denied rebates, we began to wonder if this wasn't a concerted practice to increase profits. We're sure it isn't, but Sprint's rebate process needed an overhaul. Better yet, it should eliminate rebates and simply discount the price of the phones. Why do wireless providers use rebates, then make it challenging to qualify? In marketing, there is a term referred to as "slippage," which means that a good number of customers intend to send in for the rebate but don't.

The health insurance industry uses the three D's to keep its costs down: deny, delay and defend. This is a well-documented fact. If you search "deny, delay, defend" in Google, you will see there are numerous results. First, the insurance companies deny your claim and hope you go away. Then, they delay action on your requests. Last, if you push a claim, they use lawyers to defend against paying you, because they know most consumers don't have the funds or know how to legally defend their rights. Andersen Cooper of CNN conducted an 18-month investigation of this practice. This is a major reason why the 2010 health care bill was passed.

We were denied coverage in 2009 by Assurant Health, a Time Insurance Company. It invited us to change to a policy with the company, then denied us coverage. It also placed an exclusion on Lynn for varicose veins. This is why passage of the health care bill was so critical — to stop these unfair practices by giant insurance companies. Think about it ... an insurance company invites us to apply for a new policy, then denies us and excludes Lynn for varicose veins.

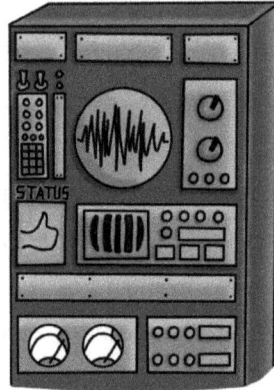

"REP-RE-SENT-A-TIVE"

"Oh, brother!"

"Tell me what you would like."

"Where would you like to send the package?"

Chapter 10
Just Plain Dumb Business Practices

W E included this example to highlight incompetent accounting, and also to recognize a fine customer service oriented organization: CheckFree.

We are early adopters regarding technology and like to try new things. In January 1994, we began using Quicken and paying our bills electronically. Today that doesn't seem like a big deal, but it was pretty "out there" in 1994. As far as we are aware, no banks offered online banking at that time.

The way it worked in 1994 was as follows. A company named CheckFree had a marketing arrangement with Intuit, the makers of Quicken. CheckFree was in the business of paying bills for companies and began moving into the consumer arena. We signed up with CheckFree for bill paying. We would submit the payments online via Quicken, and CheckFree would pay our bills and debit our checking account. Some payments would be made electronically, and others, the old-fashioned way, with a paper check — the same as it is today. The cost was about the same as buying postage, except we didn't have to lick anything or worry about payments arriving late. Today, this service through your bank is usually free.

We were skeptical at first, because the descriptions used in the digital world back then (and now) — turnkey, drop in, fail-safe — never seemed to prove true. As we got used to this process of paying our bills, we found it worked perfectly. Moreover, CheckFree had outstanding customer service and this alleviated our fears. We've included examples on the following pages of its excellent service.

In January 1997, we received our quarterly sewer and water bill from Sanitary District No. 4, where we live. We looked at the due date, and entered it into Quicken to be paid on that day. That was a feature we appreciated, that you get to hold onto your money until the last possible day. After using Quicken and CheckFree for three years, we encountered our first problem. We received a late notice from Sanitary District No. 4, saying it hadn't received our payment and a late fee was added. Until we resolved the issue, we immediately sent them a paper check, including payment of the late fee along with a letter. Our sanitary district told us that they couldn't process payments on the day they were received and, therefore, our payment was posted late and we were charged a finance charge.

This further illustrates the need for organizations to hire better people and take personal responsibility. The following e-mails between ourselves, CheckFree and Sanitary District No. 4 explain the chronology of events.

Feb. 28, 1997

Sanitary District No. 4
2340 American Drive
Neenah, WI 54956

To Whom It May Concern:

Enclosed is payment for our bill of $131.76, which includes a late charge. We pay our bills electronically via CheckFree and it shows payment was made on 2/17 for $127.92. I am following up with CheckFree on this. If payment was already made to you by CheckFree, I would expect a refund of the payment and late fee.

Regards,
Thomas E. Wilson

To: CheckFree Corp.
From: Tom Wilson
Re: Sanitary District No. 4, $127.92 payment on 2/17/97

Dear CheckFree Corp.:

I contacted Sanitary District No. 4 today (2/28) and it does not show a payment. You show a confirmation number BABH-6509-5838 on 2/17 that the payment was made. Would you please check into this? I am going to send a paper check in the meantime.

Sincerely,
Thomas E. Wilson

To: Thomas Wilson
From: CheckFree Customer Care

Thank you for your inquiry regarding your 02/17/97 payment to Sanitary District No. 4, account no. XXXX. The check we sent for you was written against CheckFree's corporate account and it cleared on 02/21/97. Since the check has been cashed, it may be that Sanitary District No. 4 needs more time to post the payment to your account. If you find the funds have not been credited to your account on your next statement, please contact us so that we can resolve this for you.

To: CheckFree Corp.
From: Thomas E. Wilson
Re: Sanitary District No. 4, $127.92 payment on 2/17/97

Dear CheckFree Corp.:

I sent you an e-mail on this on 2/28. You responded on 3/3, saying payment had been made and the check cleared. They cannot find a record of such payment. Please provide a copy of both sides of the cancelled check.

Sincerely,
Thomas E. Wilson

March 17, 1997

To: Thomas Wilson
From: CheckFree Customer Care

Thank you for your 03/15/97 inquiry regarding your $127.92 to Sanitary District No. 4, due 02/17/97. We have verified that we issued the payment as scheduled. So that we can help resolve this for you, we will contact Sanitary District No. 4 to determine why the payment has not been posted to your account. We will contact you with a resolution as soon as possible.

March 18, 1997

To: Thomas Wilson
From: CheckFree Customer Care

We are writing in response to your inquiry regarding the following payment:

Merchant: Sanitary District No. 4
Amount: $173.10
Scheduled Payment Date: 02/17/97

Sanitary District No. 4 advised us your payment still has not posted to your account. However, we discovered that your payment was inadvertently posted to another account. We are sending documentation asking the merchant to credit your account and waive any fees that resulted from the disposing. Please allow Sanitary District No. 4 10 business days to research and apply this payment. I spoke with Pat and she stated she would discuss the late fees with you; she would not waive them for me.

March 20, 1997

To: CheckFree
From: Thomas E. Wilson

Dear CheckFree Corp.:

This responds to the e-mail you sent me about a payment to Sanitary District No. 4. I also spoke to Pat and she told me I would be charged the late fee because the fault was with CheckFree. Apparently, CheckFree issues one check to merchants, along with an attached ledger indicating which accounts should be credited. She told me the ledger didn't indicate our account number. I find this hard to believe. Would you have a copy of this that I could share with her?

Sincerely,
Thomas E. Wilson

March 25, 1997

To: Thomas Wilson
From: CheckFree Customer Care

Thank you for your recent inquiry. I spoke with Paula, the office manager at Sanitary District No. 4, about the late fees on your 2/17 payment for $127.92. I advised her that four pages were faxed over to the attention of Pat, including the remittance. I advised her also that this is what the original remittance would have looked like. She believes they never received this.

I then advised her it clearly says on the check to call our merchant services department if this paper is missing. I advised her to call this number in the future if there is ever a problem regarding a check she receives from CheckFree. Paula stated she had already spoken with you and waived the late fees. She reiterated these fees were waived. If you have a question, please feel free to call Customer Care at 800-297-3180 8 a.m. to midnight, EST, Monday through Friday.

Thank you for using CheckFree!

Following is our final correspondence with Sanitary District No. 4. At the time, the town had the sanitary district set up as its own little kingdom, along with its own president — this, in a very small town. Who's heard of a president of a sanitary district? When we did finally receive the refund, they forgot to include the late fee or, for that matter, an apology. We had to follow up again.

Sometime after March 25, 1997

Sanitary District No. 4

To Whom It May Concern:

I recently received a check from you (#1583 dated 3/20/97) in the amount of $127.92. Please send a check for the late fee that I paid on 3/14/97. As you can see, the original payment was made on time. This has taken an incredible amount of our time. Please let me know if you have any questions.

Regards,
Thomas E. Wilson

To make sure "Mr. President" knew what was going on, Tom sent him this letter:

March 26, 1997

Mr. John Doe
President, Sanitary District No. 4
2340 American Drive
Neenah, WI 54956

Dear Mr. Doe:

The purpose of this letter is to request a late fee refund of $3.84. On 2/17/97, I made payment on our account XXXX in the amount of $127.92. This payment is made on our behalf by CheckFree Corp.

Following this payment, I received a late notice in the amount of $131.76, which included the $127.92 and a late fee of $3.84. I made this payment on 3/14/97 from our personal checking account immediately and sent a letter.

At the same time, I e-mailed CheckFree to let them know that you said you never received our payment. They checked into it and e-mailed me back.

Regards,
Thomas E. Wilson

Tom included all the e-mails between ourselves, CheckFree and Sanitary District No. 4, so the district president could see firsthand the confusion this caused and the amount of time it took to straighten out. He never offered an apology, or for that matter, a response. I guess customer service isn't a requirement in the sanitary business; he forgot who was paying his salary.

As a reminder, the correspondence is included to show how best to communicate issues to companies and organizations.

Dry Cleaning

Following is a simple example about handling clothing damaged at a dry-cleaning facility. In the example below, a shirt that a dry cleaner damaged was a year old, so when we deducted for it, we subtracted one-third from the original cost, feeling the life of a dress shirt is about three years. Our contact with the dry-cleaning business was concise, specific and direct.

May 4, 1997

So's Dry Cleaning
404 E. Kimberly Ave.
Kimberly, WI 54136

To Whom It May Concern:

Enclosed is a receipt for a short-sleeve shirt that was damaged. Because the shirt is a year old, I have subtracted one-third of the original cost of $71.40 (includes tax). Therefore, the current value of the shirt is $47.84. Our current bill dated April 30 (included) shows a balance of $25.47. I am subtracting the present value of the damaged shirt leaving a credit (to me) of $22.37, which should be included on your next invoice to me. Please advise if you have any questions.

Regards,
Tom Wilson

The dry cleaner accepted this deduction after we had a small debate about the original cost of the shirt. In some cases, like this one, it's easier to deduct what you feel a company owes you than to debate it and wait for a check, which could be a long process and necessitate more follow-up on your part. You have much more leverage when you deduct. It is also helpful to charge your purchases, because then you can go through your credit card company, explaining why you deducted. The credit card companies simply charge back the merchant until the issue is resolved.

Don't ever feel sorry for banks and credit card companies. They make the small merchants pay for disputed merchandise returns and fraudulent purchases made with stolen credit cards, even after they approve purchases with merchants and provide them with approval codes. We learned this firsthand with our startup business, The CareGiver Partnership. The credit card companies are never left holding the bag.

Landscape Stone

This is another fairly straightforward example. When our home was constructed in 1990, we purchased brick from a landscape company. As part of the purchase incentive, we were to receive a 10 percent discount on all future purchases.

Nine years later, we ordered landscape fabric and stone and reminded the company about our discount. When the stone was delivered, the fabric was not included, although it was charged it to our credit card. Tom had to call, remind the company about our discount and point out the missing fabric. They at first gave him a hard time, insisting the fabric had indeed been delivered.

This was a simple order that resulted in two mistakes and the need for us to call and write a letter. We almost always write letters because it creates a record. Phone messages are easily lost or forgotten.

May 1999

Fox Valley Stone and Brick Co., Inc.
1745 Breezewood Lane
Neenah, WI 54956

Dear Andy:

This follows up on your phone call to me last Friday, May 7, regarding payment of the attached invoice. You should have received payment in full for this.

Since we bought the brick for our house from you, I was told we would get a 10 percent discount on future purchases. This wasn't reflected on the invoice. Also, the landscape fabric was never delivered. Therefore, would you please send me a refund check for $50.35 based on the following?

$360.00 @ 10% discount = $36.00
Landscape fabric = $11.95
Tax on above = $2.40

Let me know if you have any questions.

Sincerely,
Thomas E. Wilson

We ultimately received the payment, but the situation left a bad taste in our mouths. We never again did business with the company and have purchased a great deal more stone and supplies elsewhere.

Office Max Rebate

Tom went to Office Max one day to take advantage of an offer on CDs that included a hefty rebate. The store had run out of the advertised product but substituted another equivalent brand for the same price. When we sent in for our rebate, we knew it was in our best interest to include a note to this effect, to prevent another denied rebate. Many companies outsource rebate processing to other organizations. Since many want as few consumers as possible to actually get rebates, they often allow their surrogates to harass consumers by denying submissions that don't have every I dotted and T crossed. In the end, while this may save a few dollars, it makes consumers furious.

Note the second paragraph of the following letter, regarding time lines that are neither fair nor a customer-friendly policy.

OfficeMax February Cash Offer

Dept. 03-70430
P.O. Box 540005
El Paso, TX 88554-0005

To Whom It May Concern:

Our local store (ZIP code 54956, Appleton, Wisconsin) ran out of the Radiate CDs and substituted Imation, which I was told would carry the $20 rebate.

It is interesting to note you only allow your customers 14 days to send in the rebates, but allow yourself 56 days to mail the checks — four times as long. You have to ask yourself, is that customer oriented?

Please contact the store should you have any questions.

Regards,
Tom Wilson

Hello, Marketing Department? Is Anyone Home?

Sometimes we see plain inept marketing and Tom knows he'll always have a job in marketing. It may not be a good job, but there will always be one. Our classic example is a billboard in Waco, Texas, that advertised a substance abuse program. The only words on the billboard were, "The First Step Is to Call." It didn't include a phone number.

We suspect many of you have heard of Masco or its Behr Division. It's a gold-standard example of how to successfully resolve an issue with a customer. We have a positive image of this company and go out of our way to select its products.

During April 2004, we were at our local Home Depot, looking for faux-finish materials for a powder room. We asked for assistance and, true to form, the Home Depot associate was well versed on the subject. Upon completing his explanation of a technique, he presented us with a brochure from the manufacturer of the product. The brand, Behr, was manufactured by Masco Corp.

We looked over the brochure at home, and one of its copy points described a free CD on faux-finishing techniques using its products. We searched the brochure to find how to obtain a copy, but there was no indication on how to do so. We went on the company's Web site and still could not determine how to obtain a copy. We contacted the company via its site and asked for a copy to be sent to our home.

The next day, we received a reply saying we would have to contact the customer service area to request one. We e-mailed back, saying that

"Never underestimate the power of the irate customer."

since they *are* the company, we would have expected them to take care of that for us. Regardless, we contacted customer service and requested a copy. It was at that point we found out the CD was not free. We had to either purchase it at Home Depot or directly through the company. We were further notified that Home Depot didn't have any yet because they were running "behind," but "should" have them "shortly."

Read the letter below for additional background. Then we'll share with you how this was successfully resolved.

April 16, 2004

Mr. Richard A. M.
Chairman and CEO
Masco Corp.
21001 VanBorn Road
Taylor, MI 48180

Dear Mr. M.:

The purpose of this letter is to bring to your attention what I consider a misleading marketing practice by your Behr Division.

This division distributes point-of-sale materials regarding faux textures within Home Depot. The materials include a copy point stating, "Find out how easy and fun it is to create your own faux finishes. To see inspirational results on how to turn ordinary walls into extraordinary works of art, look for our interactive CD-ROM: Faux Finishing Techniques." The only problem is, where do I look for it?

I took the time to visit Behr's Web site and couldn't find out how to order it. I finally contacted Behr's customer service department via your Web site and requested a copy. After receiving a reply that I would have to call to order one, I asked that since I'd taken the time to contact the company, wouldn't someone please arrange it for me? I received a reply that the CD isn't complimentary; we would have to pay for it. After all that, the facts come out. Why would I pay for a CD that promotes your product? It's called consumer promotion.

This practice is substandard marketing, at best. If you print an offer in your brochure, you ought to tell consumers how they can obtain it. For example, consider adding, "You can purchase a copy at any Home Depot or send $X to ..."

Since we've taken the time to point this out, perhaps you could send me a free copy so I can view it, go to our local Home Depot and purchase your product?

Best regards,
Tom Wilson
C: Mr. Bob N., chairman, president and CEO, Home Depot

When we write letters, we often like to copy others who may be influential in speeding things along. In this case, we were pretty sure that Masco/Behr didn't want to upset the Home Depot CEO or his buyers and merchandisers. It wants to have a quick, positive resolution.

The company handled the situation well, responding to Tom in a timely manner. The president of the Behr division called our home and seemed genuinely interested in Tom's comments. At the end of the conversation, he asked what he could do. We don't ask for handouts and Tom told him he just wanted to point out an area he thought they could enhance. He thanked Tom and asked if he could send a complimentary copy of the CD to us, which we thought was great and thanked him. By the way, the CD was very well done.

FedEx Kinko's, Now FedEx Office

We really wonder how Kinko's stays in business. We had four interactions with the company, and on three of the four occasions, there were serious problems — all, we believe, directly related to human error. We no longer use Kinko's.

By way of background, Kinko's was acquired by Federal Express in the early part of 2004. As you read the letter Tom wrote to the CEOs of Kinko's and FedEx, keep in mind the FedEx Kinko's advertising slogan: "Relax, it's FedEx."

June 11, 2004

Mr. Gary M. K.
Chief Executive Officer
Kinko's Inc.
Three Galleria Tower
13155 Noel Road, Suite 1600
Dallas, TX 75240

Dear Mr. K.:

The purpose of this letter is to make you aware of service issues at Kinko's in Appleton, Wisconsin. I believe your FedEx unique selling proposition is "Relax, it's FedEx." Unfortunately, based on my experience, nothing could be further from reality. I absolutely, positively don't trust or rely on the Kinko's, or the now rebranded FedEx Kinko's service. Let me explain and I believe you'll understand why.

In April, I began using Kinko's for our business needs. Since then, we've had four opportunities to use the service and experienced three major issues.

April 12

I e-mailed a PowerPoint presentation to have five copies printed. I arrived at the store at the appointed time to pick them up. I provided my name and told the associate I had e-mailed the presentation and was instructed to pick it up at this time. I was told there was no process of knowing when orders were transmitted electronically and, therefore, the project hadn't been started. *(Note: This is a deficiency in providing employees with the proper tools to deliver on management's service promise.)*

I said I would wait for the order to be printed and waited about 45 minutes. I had provided special covers and back sheets to be included with the spiral binding. When the work was completed, those weren't included. I waited while the presentations were unbound and then rebound.

May 11

Realizing I couldn't depend on e-mailing a print job to Kinko's, I dropped off the next project. The presentation was pulled off my CD, loaded onto a Kinko's computer, then checked. I left report covers and back pages to be bound as part of the job. When I returned the next day at 9 a.m., I learned the associate had written the wrong date on the job jacket and it hadn't been started. She said Kinko's would print it and deliver it to our home.

After it arrived at 5 p.m., I brought it into our house for inspection and found the entire presentation had been spiral-bound backwards. I called the store, and the driver returned and took the presentations back to be reworked. They were unbound, rebound and returned the next morning.

June 6

At this point, I am anticipating errors and have modified our time lines to accommodate them. On this occasion, I needed five copies of three presentations printed and spiral bound with our unique covers. I also needed color copies of a magazine advertisement printed and shipped via FedEx. I didn't have the address with me, so I told the associate I would call him the next day with it, which I did.

I had arranged that the presentations be shipped by FedEx overnight. On June 8, I called the client and found they hadn't been shipped on June 7 as promised. I called the store, explaining our displeasure and asked for a refund on the shipping. I was told to call FedEx since Kinko's isn't responsible for shipping. What is the point of a merger if there isn't any benefit for the customer?

These examples clearly indicate significant room for improvement. All the associates I worked with were pleasant and I believe they wanted to deliver good work and excellent customer service. Most of the errors highlighted above were human error. Better recruiting and enhanced training likely would lead to improved results.

I would like our account credited for the shipment mentioned above. Our account number and contact information follows.

I am working on a book about customer service and I plan to include this example. If you have any comments on enhancements you plan to make in the near future that you would like me to consider including, please let me know.

Best regards,
Tom Wilson
C: Mr. Frederick W. S., chairman, president and CEO, FedEx

We received a reply from a woman at FedEx's Customer Advocate Desk. She left a message with a phone number; however, the phone number was a general customer service number that put Tom right back into the telephone maze with its automated list of voice-activated questions. He tried several times to speak slowly and clearly, repeating the word "representative." The response he received asked if he wanted to send a package. Frustrated and out of time, he decided to try again later.

Now, what's wrong with this picture? We had suffered through three problems with FedEx Kinko's and had taken the time to write to both of its leaders, FedEx and Kinko's, explaining in detail our issues and that we were planning to include them in our book. Obviously, our letter didn't faze them a bit, because they routinely turned our issue over to the Customer Advocate Desk. We don't have a problem with this. What we do have a problem with is that when a company calls, it should provide a direct line to return the call. As explained above, we couldn't get through the automated system. This is a prime example of where systems and technology are installed to reduce costs, yet hurt customer service. Of course the leaders of FedEx and Kinko's will probably never have to experience this. If they have an issue with a company, they have assistants handle it.

On June 28, 2004, we received the following e-mail from the same woman at FedEx. We've duplicated the actual e-mail here, in all its glory, including the lack of formatting, incorrect grammar and misspelled words. When we went to school, you capitalized the first word in a sentence and a person's last name. We're pretty sure they haven't changed the rules, but for some reason, people think that anything goes when sending e-mails. That's bad business, as it reflects poorly on an organization's image. In this case, if you have sloppy grammar, maybe you have sloppy service, which we experienced.

---

dear mr wilson,

i have left several mesages for you regarding your experience at our kinko's location. please give me a call at 800-463-XXXX ask for the customer advocate desk in dallas texas, My name is: (name excluded) or email me with a telephone number where you can be reached to discuss.

When companies began using typewriters in their communications, they didn't throw away the good grammar rule book. Communicating articulately and clearly in e-mail is just as important as it is in verbal communication. Business leaders have to get on top of this, so their hard-earned images do not suffer.

Back to the FedEx Kinko's example. Tom called again and received FedEx's regular phone number, saying it would be closed on Independence Day. His call then was placed into its phone queue labyrinth. This time, however, he successfully made it through to customer service. The person who answered had to look up our "Customer Advocate's" phone number because she was located in a different state. Once connected to her office, Tom was put on hold while she located our information.

Here is a key point worth repeating: When a consumer or customer takes the time to contact you, please provide a direct number to get back in touch with you. How would you like it if your Customer Advocate called consumers and was put on hold and expected to go through a maze of choices to get to us consumers? We think you would find it time consuming (read: expensive) and frustrating. Guess what? We consumers do too. Also, think about the cost of a customer having to talk with two of your people before reaching the right person. That is not efficient.

When Tom finally did make contact with the FedEx Customer Advocate, she did a marvelous job. It was apparent she was experienced, spoke excellent English, was empathetic, apologized twice for the problems and offered to credit our account for the delayed shipment. She also said she would be sending a complimentary coupon for his troubles. Further, she told Tom that FedEx was working through integration issues with Kinko's employees and was trying to get them up to speed as quickly as possible.

This brings us to an important point, and one you should remember as a consumer. When two companies merge, the customer can up short in some cases, at least within the first year of the merger. The reason is, in the excitement of what's referred to as "doing the deal," some CEOs get excited about the publicity they'll receive and the effects it may have on their companies' stock prices, as well as the increase in the value of their stock options. They often don't take sufficient time to really think through the integration issues or commit sufficient resources to ensure success.

The merger of Hewlett-Packard and Compaq was well publicized and very contentious. In mathematics, two negative numbers added together result in a larger negative number. The headstrong CEO of HP decided that new math applied to the acquisition of Compaq by HP. She sold the concept that if she combined the unprofitable HP computer business with the unprofitable Compaq computer business, it would become a real money maker.

That may sound silly, but the HP board rolled over and let her do just that. Then the company layed off thousands of workers, outsourced work to India, and at the same time ordered not one but two $30 million Gulfstream private jets. We're glad we didn't own the stock. The stock price had been nearly $75 per share. Five years later, following her brilliant merger, it was $18. By 2008, the stock price lost about 40 percent of its value. She ultimately was fired by the board and, in her arrogant demeanor, claimed she has "no regrets." Tens of thousands of stockholders, employees and consumers certainly did. Now she wants to be in government.

In the FedEx Kinko's example, Fed Ex acquired Kinko's and created an end-to-end service under the advertising slogan, "Relax, it's FedEx." As is usually the case, not enough strategic planning, resources or energy went into the implementation phase. A detailed operational plan against which to execute clearly wasn't properly developed. A FedEx employee from "corporate" admitted to me they were working through issues and were trying to get the Kinko's people trained.

This brings us to another reality: If the company you work for acquires another company, that's good because you're smart and don't need incremental training. If you work for the acquired company, you're going to find that you're a little short on skills and you will likely require training to get you "up to speed." You are a "legacy" employee and likely will not fare well in the new structure.

Our last example is a sad one. A man who was CEO of a midsized company that manufactured and distributed products for incontinence and other absorbent products developed "visions of grandeur" in his mid to late 50s. He was running a family-owned business his father founded years before, when he decided he wanted to become a big player in the industry and bought two other companies in a relatively short period of time. One was the incontinence business from Procter & Gamble, which was the Attends brand; the other, a less-recognized name.

There was only one problem: He tried to integrate too quickly, and because the three companies' systems weren't compatible, they couldn't take, process or ship orders. The company melted down, the banks took over, and soon placed a "turnaround artist" inside to cut costs and sell it. The CEO whose company his father had started found himself out of a job.

Our advice to consumers is to avoid doing business with any company that in the previous year has merged or been acquired. You're likely to encounter poor service, because much of the time, the operating people on the front lines are the last to find out what the strategy is. Often they haven't received proper training, staffing or the tools to deliver on the integration.

Our advice to business owners is to recognize this fact and include funding in your acquisition plan to hire or maintain sufficient staff and provide training on the new company mission, procedures and products, well before implementation. Two common and fatal merger mistakes are assuming there will be more synergies than turns out to be, and assuming the growth targets of the combined organizations will be achieved. In the business world, "synergies" is one of those happy-talk words, similar to "collateral damage" used by the military. It makes reality sound nicer. Synergies often really means firing redundant workers, closing plants and outsourcing functions.

As a businessperson, the initial synergies may not look as enticing at the proposal stage, but your stockholders and certainly customers will benefit in the longer run if you properly staff, train, and provide tools to your team to execute the growth strategy plan your board and investment bankers viewed. A scorched-earth policy to maximize synergies from day one is a big mistake.

306 Days of Failure

On May 25, 2003, Tom purchased a wireless headset to work with his cell phone. Using a cell phone and trying to jot notes is challenging, as we all know. It's much easier to talk hands-free. Tom liked the concept of wireless and, as he viewed the package in the store, he was careful to ensure the model was compatible with his cell phone.

Tom took it home and started using it, and found sometimes it would work properly, but mostly it either didn't work at all or had a great deal of static. He phoned the company and told someone about the problem. The customer service representative asked what type of phone he had, then said it wasn't compatible, even though the package said it was. The rep agreed to send out a new compatible model. Following is the letter Tom sent with the headset.

Dec. 19, 2003

Plantronics
345 Encinal St.
Santa Cruz, CA 95060

Attn: Warranty Express

Enclosed please find a model M1500 headset purchased May 25, 2003, from Best Buy. I have not been able to successfully get the headset to work properly. There is a great deal of interference (static) while on a call, unless I literally hold the phone next to the headset. My phone is a Samsung SPH-N300 dual-band phone with Sprint.

Please either repair or replace this headset. Thank you in advance.

Regards,
Tom Wilson

Tom waited quite a while for the new headset to arrive and had to call to check its status. Once it did finally arrive, he connected it to his phone and found it didn't work any better. He called the company again, and after providing the phone's make and model, was told it wasn't compatible.

He packaged up the headset right away and sent it back, along with the following letter.

Feb. 6, 2004

Ms. Alisa M.
Plantronics Service
345 Encinal St.
Santa Cruz, CA 95060

Dear Ms. M.:

Per your instructions, I am returning a M1500 cordless headset for a refund, as it is not compatible with my Samsung SPH-N300 phone.

Enclosed is my purchase receipt of the original unit for $79.99 plus $4 sales tax. I had contacted Plantronics in December, and you asked that I return that headset. I did so, and you then shipped me the headset I am now returning. Therefore, I have spent an additional $8.24 to ship the original unit back to you, including postage insurance, and have spent the same or a similar amount on this shipment. Therefore, my total investment in your product is $100.47. I would like a check for this amount.

I am disappointed that your headset didn't work. It is unfortunate that the carton doesn't indicate which models the headset will work with. It is also unfortunate that when I called, Plantronics sent me another M1500, even though I had indicated the make and model of the phone I planned to use it with.

Alisa, thanks for your help over the phone last week with this, and thank you in advance for your help resolving this.

Best regards,
Tom Wilson

Almost two months later, on March 29, 2004, Tom had to call Ms. M. to ask about the status of the refund. That same day, he received a call from someone who apologized for the delay, saying he "should" receive the refund "shortly." He received the check on April 1, 2004, exactly 306 days after making the initial purchase, and after calling a number of times and sending back two units.

Lessons learned: There were a number of problems with Plantronics. Its packaging certainly wasn't clear. Its customer service needed significant improvement in tools and systems. Tom found its people easy to deal with, but there were too many mistakes along the way that could have been avoided.

Luckily throughout the process, Tom maintained the purchase receipt and a chronology of all correspondence, including names, dates, phone numbers and follow-up action. While he ultimately received a refund, it was a long, painful process. We would be skeptical purchasing another Plantronics product.

Real Simple (Really?)

Real Simple is a magazine about simplifying your life. Let us share with you how it made its ordering process anything but simple.

In December 2003, our oldest daughter purchased two subscriptions as Christmas gifts, for her mother-in-law and for her friend. She e-mailed her subscription order, charging it to her debit card. Because she knew it would take six to eight weeks to start receiving monthly issues, she purchased two newsstand copies to give as gifts, announcing the subscription would begin in February or March.

In late December, she received one copy in error at her home. She e-mailed the publisher, saying she had mistakenly received a copy. By mid-March, neither gift recipient had begun receiving the magazine. Our daughter e-mailed the publisher a second time and received an e-mail response saying that due to unusually high demand, there was a shortage, but that they should be receiving the magazine within four to six weeks.

By mid-April, she followed up again via e-mail. The customer service representative looked up her record and said it "should" begin soon. By June 13, the subscription hadn't yet begun, a full six months since it was first ordered. So this is how Real Simple magazine delivers customer service. It charged our daughter's credit card as soon as she subscribed, but never bothered to contact her when it couldn't deliver.

Lessons learned: What should have happened? First, as soon as the publisher knew the publication was in trouble, someone should have credited our daughter's card until it could deliver. At the same time, the company should have contacted her to inform her of the situation. They did neither. In our opinion, this is almost criminal. If this happened to us, we would immediately cancel the subscription, in writing, and contact the appropriate authorities and trade groups. This organization hasn't earned and doesn't deserve our daughter's hard-earned money. By the way, Real Simple is a Time Inc. publication — it should have known better.

Following is the correspondence on this issue.

Kristiana:

Thanks for getting back to me so promptly. I forwarded your e-mail to our daughter. In the meantime, her contact information is: _____.

Regards,
Tom Wilson

"One customer well taken care of could be more valuable than $10,000 worth of advertising."

From: Kristiana H.
Sent: Wednesday, June 16, 2004, 7:21 p.m.
To: Tom Wilson
Subject: Your note to Real Simple

Dear Mr. Wilson:

Thank you so much for writing Real Simple on Sunday. I apologize for the delay in responding; I was traveling and unable to write back until I returned today. I was very sorry to hear of your daughter's problems with customer service — it's not what we strive for, and I deeply apologize. (*This is good. She provided an apology; so many companies don't.*) I would like to follow up with you and her on this matter. Could you forward me her full name and address so I can look up her account? Of course we can credit her account and give her a free subscription in its place. While it appears this should have happened immediately, it's certainly the least I can do now.

I would love to solve this problem, speak to you and your daughter about what happened in this specific situation, and talk about ways we can do better in the future. Is this possible? If so, I look forward to receiving your daughter's full name and address. If you would prefer to talk on the phone, please call collect. Our number is 212-XXX-XXXX.

Many thanks,
Kristiana H.
Consumer Marketing Director
Real Simple

The magazine followed up with another e-mail to Tom on June 21, 2004, saying it hadn't been able to make contact with our daughter. During that week, our daughter made contact. The person she spoke with was polite and apologetic, and admitted there was no record of her contacting them previously. Moreover, as far as the magazine's records showed, our daughter's three subscriptions were being fulfilled.

In the end, our daughter received an apology and three complimentary subscriptions to begin in July 2004.

Lessons learned: This was a good response — timely, apologetic and an offer of a free subscription to make up for the errors, which is reasonable given all the follow-up required and the fact that two of the three were gifts. Of course, what's really ironic about this example is the situation tied together with the name of the magazine: Real Simple. (Really?)

This issue could have been prevented if the company had better systems that kept track of all customer interaction, as well as the ability to proactively reach out to customers when there was an issue, such as being oversold. At The CareGiver Partnership, we keep track of every customer interaction, whether it's via phone, mail or online. When a customer contacts us, we have a complete record of everything we've talked with them about and anything they mailed us or information we've mailed to them.

Advertising at the Movies

This is a business practice that really bothers us and many other consumers. The movie theater business has had its ups and downs over time. With large format, high-definition television and surround sound, consumers now have a movie theater experience at home. Some of the screens in smaller theaters are not much larger than the largest big-screen home televisions.

With this in mind, why would theater owners want to aggravate their customers by forcing them to watch advertising? Especially when theaters continually increase the prices of tickets and refreshments. In theaters, we've experienced as many as four commercials. Annoying enough, but the bigger issue is showing the movie using a blown soundboard, and, as a result, the sound is very loud. We were not told this when we purchased the tickets or before the movie started. Following is the letter we sent to the CEO of the theater chain.

Mr. M.
Chairman and CEO
Marcus Theaters
Milwaukee, WI

Dear Mr. M.:

I'm writing to make you aware of our dissatisfaction with your company's theater operation in Appleton, Wisconsin. I have two customer service issues:

- Poor-quality sound

- Showing commercials prior to the movie

Background

On Saturday afternoon, Nov. 23, my wife and I went to the 4 p.m. showing of "Die Another Day." When the commercials, previews and show started, the sound was very, very loud. At first I thought the sound was turned up for the commercials. However, 10 minutes into the movie, it was apparent that something was wrong. I left the theater and asked your assistant manager if there was a problem. He told me the soundboard was blown. I suggested he might have announced this to customers prior to the show beginning and offered to provide passes for another showing. My guess is there were some customers who thought this was normal.

I also suggested, in a nice way, that showing four commercials prior to a movie was excessive. He became indignant and said, "We have nothing to do with that. They make a ton of money on the commercials, and unless a couple of hundred thousand people call, nothing's going to change." I told him I was just mentioning it to him to pass it along. His attitude was so poor, I asked for, and received, a refund and drove to another theater to see the movie.

What should have happened? There should have been an announcement that there was a problem. Customers could have a made a decision to stay or return later.

Not only did we not get what we expected — a movie properly shown — we had to drive to another theater. There was no "we're sorry" or "here's a coupon for free popcorn for next time." Nothing but an indignant assistant manager.

Regarding the commercials, my guess is you would tell me they help keep prices down. However, since your competitors don't follow the same practice, I will choose to visit their theaters.

Regards,
Tom Wilson

We received no response.

Lessons learned: You have to speak up. In this case, the CEO didn't care enough to acknowledge the time a long-term customer took to write, so we have a rule, which is to make sure we don't reward bad behavior. We have not visited his theater since. Thank goodness for competition.

"Politeness goes far, yet costs nothing."

"I'm sorry, but your CompleteCare coverage program does not cover theft, loss, damage, manufacturer's defects or malfunctioning devices."

Chapter 11

The Digital World

THE following examples illustrate the activities of both America Online and Dell. Their practices were found to be illegal by the government. More importantly, they are both just bad business practices. Executives at these companies have no idea of the cost to stockholders' equity when they implement practices designed to maximize short-term profitability.

America Online

Today, most people don't have the foggiest idea who drove the early days of America Online. He was egotistical and arrogant, and had a major role in destroying much of the value of Time Warner. (For the record, it was AOL that acquired Time Warner, not the other way around.) For a brief period, he changed the Time Warner company name to AOL Time Warner. After the meltdown of the company due to the drag by AOL, that part of the name was dropped. During the tremendous growth of AOL, he was focused on driving growth and profit. Customer service was so bad, the company was frequently referred to as AO Hell. Following is a letter we wrote to the company about its service.

March 13, 1997

AOL Member Refunds
PO Box 511
Ogden, UT 84402-0511

To Whom It May Concern:

Please credit our account for one month. I have had terrible problems getting online, even during the day.

Who decides to make long-term loyal customers use the mail to request a refund for terrible service when you are the No. 1 online company? I expect you to refund our 32¢ stamp. MSN is looking better all the time. If there is any question whatsoever as to whether you are going to issue a refund, please cancel our three-year prepaid subscription.

Regards,
Tom Wilson
C: State Attorney General's Office

We also alerted our credit card company that AOL's service was not acceptable and that we did not intend to pay for the three years of service we had just signed up for. The following letter is self-explanatory.

Jan. 30, 1996

Reference # _____
First Bankcard Center
P.O. Box 3696
Omaha, NE 68103-0696
Subject: Disputed Charge With AOL

I have a dispute with American Online, which debited $358.80 to our account last month as a prepayment for 36 months of service. The dispute is with its service, which is totally unacceptable since it changed to a level-pricing strategy in January. It is usually not possible for me to make a connection to the service now. When I do make a connection, the service is dramatically slower. I am attempting to get AOL to reduce its charges due to the poor service.

As you may know, this is a national problem. At least one state has filed a class-action lawsuit seeking damages. Others reportedly may also file suit. American Online has announced via the media that it is going to issue refunds to select customers.

Please advise on what you feel the appropriate next steps are. I do not plan to pay this bill until the service is improved. If necessary, I will cancel the service and switch to the Microsoft Network.

Sincerely yours,
Tom Wilson

We cancelled the service with AOL. The process to accomplish this was found, in and of itself, to be a deceptive business practice by AOL, making it virtually impossible for consumers to cancel their service. It was the New York State Attorney General's Office, then led by Eliot Spitzer, that filed suit, saying AOL employees were ignoring requests to cancel service and stop billing. The incentive to ignore requests was a rewards program made available to AOL's customer service representatives. Attorneys general from other states also filed suit, and AOL paid $3 million in fines in a class-action lawsuit in 2007. AOL is virtually on the junk heap of has-been technology companies.

Lessons learned: This case may be the most amazing in this book. Here was a large, rapidly growing, successful company. The leadership's arrogance allowed the company to lock customers into service agreements until the law chased it down. The merger of AOL and Time Warner was one of the largest, at $350 billion. Here is what the CEOs of both companies, aka "masters of the universe," predicted: "... create unprecedented and instantaneous access to every form of media and to unleash immense possibilities for economic growth, human understanding and creative expression." What does that mean? It's a litany of happy talk. And from the other CEO: "This is a historic moment in which new media has truly come of age."

The trail of despair in subsequent years included countless job losses, the decimation of retirement accounts, investigations by the U.S. Securities and Exchange Commission and the Justice Department, and countless executive upheavals. Today, the combined value of the companies, which have been separated, is about one-seventh of their worth on the day of the merger.

To call the transaction the worst in history, as it is now taught in business schools, does not begin to tell the story of how some of the brightest minds in technology and media collaborated to produce a deal now regarded by many as a colossal mistake. The stockholders lost, the employees lost, and most importantly, consumers lost.

Dell's Customer Service Policies

Following are two examples of why you have to look out for yourself as it relates to Dell. The first involves "bait and switch," how Dell offered no-interest credit to consumers. The other concerns a suit filed against Dell because its customer service was so poor that New York State Attorney General Andrew M. Cuomo stated, "At Dell, customer service means no service at all."

Cuomo filed suit against Dell and its finance arm, Dell Financial Services, LP, a joint venture between Dell and Citibank. Cuomo said, "Dell's consumers were intentionally misled, and they had to pay for that privilege. I hope this lawsuit sends a message to companies large and small that delivering a product is simply not enough — the promises they make must be delivered as well."

The lawsuit accused Dell and Dell Financial Services, or DFS, of engaging in "bait and switch" financing tactics and failing to provide its customers with adequate customer service. We experienced this firsthand and will share the example a little further on.

The lawsuit also charged Dell and DFS with perpetuating numerous other deceptive business practices relating to its technical support services, promotional financing, rebate offers, and billing and collection activities.

Poor Tech Support

According to court papers, Dell deprived consumers of the technical support to which they were entitled under their warranty or service contract by:

- Repeatedly failing to provide timely on-site repair to consumers who purchased service contracts that promised on-site and expedited service.

- Pressuring consumers, including those who purchased service contracts promising on-site repair, to remove the external covers of their computers and remove, reinstall, and manipulate hardware components. We have encountered this firsthand with service contracts we purchased for both home PCs and a tape backup system for our business.

- Discouraging consumers from seeking technical support; those who called Dell's toll-free number were subjected to long wait times, repeated transfers and frequent disconnections.

- Using defective "refurbished" parts or computers to repair or replace consumers' equipment.

No-Interest Promises

The lawsuit accused Dell of luring consumers to purchase its products with advertisements that offered attractive no-interest and/or no-payment financing promotions. In practice, however, the vast majority of consumers, even those with very good credit scores, were denied these deals.

The lawsuit also alleged that DFS incorrectly billed consumers on cancelled orders, returned merchandise or accounts they did not authorize Dell to open, and then continually harassed these consumers with illegal billing and collection activities.

Although many consumers repeatedly contacted Dell or DFS to advise the company of errors, DFS did not suspend its collection activity and Dell failed to expeditiously credit consumers' accounts, even after assuring consumers it would do so. As a result, many consumers were subjected to harassing collection calls for months on end and had their credit ratings harmed.

Following are results of a survey of Dell service by a leading consumer organization.

- 32 percent of respondents who called Dell for tech support said they were on hold for an unreasonable amount of time. Further, "After consumers have endured long wait times for a representative to come to the phone, [Dell representatives] repeatedly tell them they have reached the wrong department ... [and] repeatedly transfer consumers from one representative to the next."

- 30 percent said they were transferred to several different support staff. "Although Dell's automated telephone system often allows consumers to leave a message, [representatives] repeatedly fail to return consumers' calls."

- 21 percent struggled as they wove through the automated phone system. "Many consumers who attempt to contact the technical support department by e-mail, similarly find their pleas for assistance ignored."

- Almost 10 percent of respondents who e-mailed Dell said the company never got back to them; close to half (47 percent) said the reply they did receive was not helpful.

- Only 64 percent of survey respondents said Dell fixed their computers, while 90 percent said third-party tech support successfully solved problems with their Dell computers.

The attorney general's complaint concludes that "exasperated consumers, fed up with the endless runaround and ineffective technical support, resort to paying a third party to fix their equipment ... even though it is covered by a Dell warranty or service contract."

With this as background, following is how we responded to Dell when we applied for no-interest credit and were denied without explanation.

August 2003

Dell Financial Services
Attn: Correspondence
3500A Wabley Place
Austin, TX 78728

To Whom It May Concern:

The purpose of this letter is to ask why you rejected our application for your "no pay 'til 2004" credit promotion.

Today, I went online to order a PC and noticed your offer. I signed up online and was granted credit, but rejected for your "no pay 'til 2004" promotion, with no explanation. *(I was offered high-interest credit, which was part of the basis of the attorney general's suit.)* After contacting two departments within your company, I was told that no one could tell me why I was rejected.

After probing, I was given this address and told there was no e-mail address I could write to and no phone number to contact anyone with this question.

I have not yet ordered the PC and won't until I understand specifically why you rejected our application. Our credit rating is in the 98th percentile.

Regards,
Thomas E. Wilson

Tom also sent a letter to the CEO of Dell:

Aug. 14, 2003

Mr. Michael D.
One Dell Way
Round Rock, TX 78682

Dear Mr. D.:

The purpose of this letter is to express our concern about a "bait and switch" process you are currently using to entice consumers to use Dell Financial Services credit.

I purchased a laptop online and applied for the "no pay 'til 2004" arrangement. I was rejected, even though I have a FICO score of 799.

When I called to ask why I was rejected, I was told no one could tell me because "the computer decides." After pushing for a more specific reason, I was told there was no one I could talk to that could answer that, and further, that they don't have to tell me. After pressing further, I was given an address to write to.

Attached is the "nonexplanation explanation." Not many have better credit than I do, yet I was rejected without a specific reason. This is a bad business practice and you should stop it.

I want the "no pay 'til 2004" offer. If I don't receive it, I plan to return our laptop and purchase another brand. Please let me know if you want me to return the laptop.

Regards,
Tom Wilson

Unfortunately, we didn't receive the zero-interest credit offer. Tom also never received an explanation of why he was rejected from Dell Financial Services. It is illegal to reject a person for credit without providing an explanation. Tom wouldn't have ordered the laptop, except at the time he was incredibly busy and couldn't research a new brand and our daughter needed it for college.

This unfortunate experience made us seriously distrust Dell. We go out of our way to purchase other brands. There are so many other competitors. We're frequently surprised that companies don't come close on delivering what their advertising slogans say, or what in the ad business is called their unique selling propositions, or USPs. Dell's USP is "Easy as Dell." The problem is, nothing could be further from the truth. Maybe it should be changed to "Easy as Hell." CNET online reported that a March 2004 issue of Consumer Reports included a survey of 4,100 consumers, who gave Dell 62 points out of a possible 100 for its support on desktop PCs. The online community is full of complaints about its lack of service. Some examples:

Forest of New York City (12/14/03): "I purchased a Dell Computer XP in March, and since the date of purchase I have been having problems, mainly with the hard drive. I have contacted Dell on many occasions, but their representatives are all [hard to understand]. I sent our hard drive back to Dell, but no one has contacted me."

From ConsumerAffairs.com: "Just a few years ago, we routinely recommended Dell to our readers. But based on the torrent of consumer complaints we read daily, we would have to rate Dell's customer service as abysmal, bordering on nonexistent. Equipment and pricing aside, the shortcomings in the company's Kafkaesque customer service maze render it risky territory for those who aren't computer professionals."

I love this one from Dell's Web site, highlighting its insurance, "CompleteCare" coverage for damage to your PC. The only problem is, it *excludes* theft, loss and damage due to fire or intentional damage; isn't available in all states; and you may be required to return the unit to Dell. Now that's what I call CompleteCare! It reminded me of a spoof TV spot that ran years ago on Saturday Night Live titled "Happy Fun Ball." It advertised a red, rubber fun ball that kids could play with, then listed about 20 seconds of disclaimers.

Gateway

As marketers, we have to ask ourselves, why would they have originally named the company Gateway 2000? Was there a plan to change the name to Gateway 2010 in 2000 and then Gateway 2020 in 2010? Or maybe they didn't think that far ahead and, as the year 2000 approached, they said, "Oops." It's like Ben Franklin Five and Dime, or Motel 6, meaning a room for $6 a night — they didn't think very far ahead into the future.

The following example is illustrative of a complete systems breakdown and lack of employee empowerment that led to Gateway as a company — not the brand — ceasing to exist. Gateway had been a serious contender in the personal computer business, until its business collapsed and it tried becoming a TV company. As the meltdown continued, the company was forced to shutter many of its stores and continue its demise as one of a long list of computer companies.

Gateway as a company only lasted 22 years. It sold off its division that marketed computers to small businesses, which went bankrupt. The company has yet to offer any reprieve to customers caught up in the MPC Corp. collapse, leaving hundreds of thousands of Gateway computer owners without access to support and refusing to honor system warranties. This action significantly hurt the brand.

On Aug. 2, 1999, we ordered our second Gateway PC. In the online shipping instructions, we specifically said not to deliver it before Aug. 18, as we would be on vacation. To summarize, Gateway shipped two complete systems and a third CPU while we were on vacation and charged them to our credit card. Tom phoned to have the extra computer system and third CPU picked up. Gateway expected him to drive 30 miles to return the incorrectly shipped units. Moreover, it refused to credit our card until the incorrectly shipped units were returned and checked to make sure they were in perfect condition, even though the shipping error was Gateway's fault.

Following is the e-mail correspondence so you can understand what transpired.

Sept. 2, 1999

Mr. Theodore W.
Chief Executive Officer
Gateway
4545 Towne Center Court
San Diego, CA 921212

Dear Mr. W.:

I know how busy you must be. I also know you will find the five minutes spent reading this worthwhile.

The purpose of this letter is to make you aware of service that is so totally unacceptable, you may find it difficult to believe that it occurred in your organization. First, let me say I am a Gateway proponent and 100 percent brand loyal. I've been a customer for six years, purchasing two decked-out systems and making many Gateway recommendations to friends and co-workers.

Our issue is simple: I ordered a system via the Internet and received immediate confirmation that two *different* systems had been ordered. I tried in vain to let your organization know I only ordered and wanted one system.

Two different systems and a third CPU were delivered to our home. I immediately called Gateway, on Aug. 20, to make arrangements to return the system I didn't order. I repeatedly said I wanted to make sure the incorrect system was not charged to our credit card. Again, after repeated e-mails and phone calls, two different systems were debited to our card and have not been removed, even though I returned the system that I did not order or authorize. I want the charges removed from our credit card immediately and a confirmation that this has taken place e-mailed to me.

You may find the following worthwhile. A study conducted by Technical Assistance Research Programs, Inc., or TARP, which was commissioned by the U.S. Department of Consumer Affairs, found:

- Ninety-six percent of consumers won't let you know they are dissatisfied.

- Of these, up to 90 percent won't buy again from your company.

- You can win back up to 70 percent of customers by resolving the problem.

"Sales without customer service is like stuffing money into a pocket full of holes."

- If you handle problems quickly and well, 95 percent will become loyal customers.

Ted, you should stress the last two points within your organization. There is a reason Dell is on top, and you are slated to continue losing market share if you don't take steps now to turn around your customer service. Anyone can assemble components and put them in metal boxes; service is the key differentiator.

A chronology of events is attached.

Sincerely,
Tom Wilson

8/2/99 — I ordered a computer system via the Internet on or before 8/2, making it clear the order should not ship to arrive before 8/18.

8/2 — I received two purchase call numbers, 90809-15 and 90810-15, shortly after placing the order. The descriptions of the two systems were very different.

8/2 — I e-mailed Gateway back immediately, saying I only ordered one system. I asked that the other system be cancelled and that Gateway e-mail me back with any questions.

8/4 — Because Gateway did not respond to the first e-mail, I sent another, saying, "I am following up because I didn't receive a follow-up on this issue." Once again, Gateway did not respond to this e-mail.

8/6–8/17 — I was on vacation.

8/8 — While on vacation, I received an e-mail from Mamie B. that the (wrong) computer (order no. 39118932) would ship on 8/17.

8/16 — On or about 8/16, two different systems were delivered to our home, as well as a CPU from another customer's order. I made it very clear that the system I ordered should not be shipped to arrive before 8/18. We located the rightful owner of the extra CPU and arranged for him to pick it up.

8/17 — I returned home from vacation and phoned Gateway at once to make them aware of the errors. I was told I would receive labels for a UPS return and would need to go to UPS, about a 30-mile round trip, to ship it back to Gateway. I told the person on the phone that I wanted her to make sure our credit card was not charged due to Gateway's error. I e-mailed Mamie to say I needed UPS to pick up the system, because I shouldn't be expected to drive 30 miles to return a system that was shipped by mistake.

8/18 — Corina C. e-mailed me back, saying she is taking over from Mamie and that Gateway will "try" to have it picked up.

8/19 — Corina e-mailed me again to say she will "try" to have it picked up 8/20 and that someone would need to be home.

8/20 — Corina e-mailed me a third time to say that UPS "should" pick up today. She further insulted me by saying, "Just remember, you are responsible until the system comes back to Gateway." I responded via e-mail, "Please, let's remember who is at fault here. I am not responsible for this system. I didn't order it; you shipped it by mistake. I have gone out of my way to be honest, calling you immediately and investing at least two hours of my time arranging to have this returned to you." After having purchased a total of three Gateway systems, I don't appreciate being told I'm responsible for your mistake.

8/20 — Two separate sets of UPS return labels arrived in the mail — another error by Gateway, since only one set should have been sent. We made sure someone was home all day for the UPS pickup. It was not until Friday evening that UPS picked up the incorrect system shipped by Gateway. I provided the UPS driver with one set of return labels.

8/21 — I checked our Visa statement online and found that Gateway had charged us for both systems and no credit had been issued. I e-mailed Corina, requesting that a credit be applied to our Visa account for the system I did not order.

8/23 — Corina e-mailed me back: "I understand where you are coming from but unfortunately we cannot post any credits until we have received the system. The only thing I can recommend is to put a dispute for the charge with your credit card company. I apologize I wish we were able to put the credit back on your credit card. I have already spoke to my manager about the credit and they advise of the same we cannot put the credit until we have received the system back to Gateway." (*Note the poor grammar and punctuation in this e-mail. In our experience, companies do not train customer service employees how to properly communicate. An e-mail should display the same professionalism a letter contains.*)

8/23 — I e-mailed Corina: "I can only suggest you have your boss talk to his/her boss. If our card isn't credited tomorrow, you will have left us no other choice but to discontinue any further purchases from Gateway. I have been a steady customer since 1994 ... your call. Please let me know of your decision."

8/30 — I had not received a reply from Corina and no credit had been issued. I phoned the sales line and asked to be transferred to customer service, because I didn't want to hold for 20+ minutes by directly calling customer service. A Gateway sales representative told me he would transfer me to someone. Instead I was put on hold for 20+ minutes. I find it interesting that if you want to place an order, you generally get through much more quickly than you do if you have a service issue.

8/30 — I phoned Gateway and talked to Angie (#86419). She admitted Gateway had been experiencing problems with Internet orders getting mixed up. She determined the system I returned had been received by Gateway the afternoon of 8/30. I told Angie I was calling to have our card credited for the system that Gateway had charged without our authorization. She said it wasn't possible to apply a credit until the system had been fully inspected, which might take seven days.

Again I reminded her I did not order or authorize the system and asked to talk with her boss. After repeated denials, she finally agreed. Her boss told me it was impossible for anyone at Gateway to credit us. When asked why, she explained the complications of the administration processes inside Gateway, which is not our problem. She flippantly replied, "Then you tell me how to make it happen" and, "No one inside Gateway has the authority to approve a credit." I repeated to her that I was a loyal customer and needed this taken care of now.

Since she would not do anything for us, I asked to talk with her boss, Tim, who she said was busy. I gave her our home phone number and she said he would call at about 3:15 p.m. There was no call from Tim on 8/30, nor did he call me the following day.

9/1 — Because Tim did not return our call and our card had not been credited, I called your customer service line again at 7:30 a.m. and received the following message: "All of our customer service representatives are busy. Please call again later." Then the phone disconnected. When I finally got through, after waiting on hold for 30 minutes, I once again explained our situation to one of your associates, who said, "I can't do anything right now because we are updating our system. I'll call you back by 10 a.m." I gave her our home phone and cell numbers. Our call was finally returned at 2:45 p.m. This time I was told a credit would be issued, but it would take another five to seven business days.

9/13 — I received the following e-mail from Corina: "I show that Accounting is taking care of the order and it has processed the paperwork."

Lessons learned: This was the last computer we purchased from Gateway. As pointed out before, we don't reward bad behavior and you shouldn't either. Gateway as a company no longer exists, and the value of Gateway's brand equity has significantly declined. Its stock under its CEO tumbled from $84 per share in 1999 to $1.90 in 2007, just barely over half of the split adjusted initial public offering price of $3.75 in 1993. This is what poor customer service will do to a company in fewer than 15 years. Consumers like us voted with our pocketbooks, and didn't reward the awful service of Gateway.

"The good news is, the last renters left you some cake."

Chapter 12

Vacations: Condo and Hotel Rentals

FOLLOWING are two examples of getting less than you bargained for when renting a vacation condo or hotel room. The principals and strategies of getting your money's worth apply.

Aug. 10, 1997

RH Realty & Rentals, Inc.
6 Lagoon Road
Hilton Head Island, SC 29928

To Whom It May Concern:

The purpose of this letter is to follow up with you on the problems we encountered during our stay at the Villamare from July 26 to Aug. 2. We were very disappointed with the accommodations and are seeking at least a 15 percent credit on our Visa card — $310 — as fair compensation. This is the third time we have stayed at the Villamare and have a good idea of what to expect. The previous two occasions were with another rental agency.

Following are what caused our disappointment:

1. We could not check in until after 5 p.m. because the cleaning people and inspectors were running behind. We told them to take their time and do a good job. We waited outside the room.

2. The doorstop to room B had fallen off; we tried to fix it.

3. The hot water in the master bedroom did not work; I fixed it.

"The biggest reason positive endings don't happen is because employees are trained on policies and rules, rather than on providing excellent service."

177

4. The shower doors in both bathrooms were coated with a filthy film. The chrome along the bottom was covered with black mildew. These had obviously not been cleaned for some time.

5. There was dust and sand on the tables in the master bedroom.

6. The stove light and vanity light were burned out.

7. The closet door in the master bedroom was off its track and the mirror was filthy.

8. The metal handle on the sliding door from the master bedroom to the deck was broken in half, and my wife cut her hand on it.

9. There were crumbs and food around the glass on the dining table and behind furniture, and dead bugs behind the couch.

10. The grout around the kitchen sink was very dirty; the refrigerator door was very dirty.

11. There was half-eaten cake left in the freezer.

12. My wife ran into two live beetles and some type of crawling centipede.

13. The washing machine did not work; the agitator was broken.

14. The vacuum bag was stuffed full of hair and dust. No one had cleaned it for some time.

15. The dryer vent to the outside was packed full of lint — a fire hazard. I cleaned it out as best I could.

16. We were not able to use the pool or whirlpool for several days because the Health Department had ordered them shut down. I talked with a representative from the Health Department and she told me it was due to safety concerns.

Over the course of our stay, we noticed these problems one by one. Therefore, we did not call upon arrival. Toward the end of our stay, however, I called your office to make you aware of the problems. I requested a credit be applied to our Visa and was told I might be granted a voucher for a future stay. We are not at all interested in renting another unit from you. I was told that Rob, the manager, would be made aware of this and would call me back. Unfortunately, he never did.

On the final day of our stay, Saturday, Aug. 2, I called you at about 7 a.m. to say we were going to check out early so you would have ample time to personally inspect the premises and make the proper repairs before the next tenant arrived.

Again, a 15 percent credit to our Visa is fair, given the extremely poor conditions of the unit and our inability to use either the pool or whirlpool. Please call me if you have any questions.

Sincerely,
Thomas E. Wilson
C: Visa

Aug. 19, 1997

MBNA America
P.O. Box 15019
Wilmington, DE 19886-5019

To Whom It May Concern:

The purpose of this memo is to make you aware that I have a dispute with a payment to RH Realty & Rentals, located on Hilton Head Island, South Carolina. The amount in dispute is $300 for breach of contract on rental property. The reference number and date for the debit is 2786 on a 7/29/97 posting date; transaction date was 7/26/97. Enclosed is a check covering the remainder of our balance of $5,691.65.

Following is a copy of the letter I sent to RH Realty & Rentals concerning the dispute. This letter is a follow-up to a telephone call I made while on the premises I rented from the company.

Sincerely,
Tom Wilson

Lessons learned: We did not hear back from RH Realty. We never booked with them again. In 1997, not a lot of businesses were online. Today, it is easy to leave comments about a stay at a particular property, allowing consumers to share their experiences. Had we been able to, we would have posted ours.

Disney World

We've made many visits to Disney and wanted its CEO to be aware of some of the difficulties customers experience.

Nov. 21, 2000

Mr. Michael E.
Chief Executive Officer
Walt Disney Co.
500 S. Buena Vista St.
Burbank CA 91521

Dear Mr. E.:

This is a note to let you know how poor I think your front-end customer service is. We've been to WDW a number of times since 1975, staying at the Grand Floridian, Polynesian and Contemporary.

On our most recent experience, trying to book a simple visit for our daughters, I remembered how difficult you make it for customers to make reservations. First, I would ask you to go onto your Web site and try to find a phone number to call. Try searching "contact" or "phone" — fairly intuitive words that the average person might search.

I made a reservation for our daughters for January (reservation no. 32247915). After finding a number to call — I forget how I finally located it — I made the reservation. A payment was due Nov. 24, so I planned to call and complete the reservation with our credit card on Nov. 20.

Do you know your organization doesn't even print a reservation number on the confirmation? At the bottom of the reservation, you ask consumers to send their payments to Walt Disney Travel Co., P.O. Box 10375, etc. I would think most people want an option to book via credit card. Who has time to send a letter to a post office box and include a credit card number on it? What if a customer doesn't wish to use a personal check?

I took out our credit card to call to make the payment. Again, no phone number was listed on the reservation confirmation. I looked back in our files and located the number and noticed it wasn't a toll-free number, so I searched your Web site again. Since I couldn't find one, I used the number I had to pay for.

I told the reservationist I was calling to complete the payment. I asked her for the Disney toll-free reservation number and was told there wasn't one. Moreover, she told me that since I wasn't going to be traveling to Disney World with our daughters, who were 19 and 22, I would need to send her a letter saying I authorized the payment, even though I told her I was authorizing the payment.

Further, I told her I was completing the payment and any additional charges would be paid for by our daughters on their credit cards, which they would provide upon check-in. We discussed this for at least two minutes before I finally got her to accept our credit card number as payment.

Following are six easy steps that will help you improve customer service:

- Review your Web site from a consumer's perspective; see how cumbersome the reservation process is.

- Use intuitive search words on your site, such as "reservations," "contact" or "phone."

- Offer a toll-free number. Disney is the only entertainment organization that doesn't have one.

- Put your toll-free reservation number on your reservation confirmations. If you feel the cost savings by not offering a toll-free number supersede customer service, you should at least put one on your reservations.

- Eliminate issues with using credit cards. In our case, all I wanted to do was to buy a gift.

- Most importantly, don't make it so challenging to do business with Disney. You have a long way to go to get basic front-end customer service where it should be. In our experience, Disney is devoid of providing any type of "customer delight."

On a positive note, you have great service on the Florida WDW property. My wife and I were just there in October with our son.

Regards,
Tom Wilson

We didn't hear anything back from Mr. E. Regarding its toll-free number, Disney says it was necessary to discontinue it because it received so many calls about anything and everything related to Disney. Its toll-free number was replaced with 407-WDISNEY, a toll call. This change made it unfair to consumers who now had to spend money to talk to Disney about spending money. Every other national hospitality firm in North America has a toll-free number that anyone can call to make reservations. This speaks volumes about Disney's customer service.

Lessons learned: Don't reward bad behavior; stay somewhere else. In our opinion, Disney has become significantly overpriced relative to other high-quality entertainment venues. At minimum, when calling, ask someone to call you right back.

"At Acme Health Care Systems, we make our prices readily available if you call our rate-control department on Tuesdays between 10 and 11 a.m. We want you to be a smart health care shopper and help control costs."

Chapter 13
Medical Missteps

PILL splitting, not bill splitting. It is recognized that the end-to-end process of providing medical services in the United States is extremely inefficient. This is driven by insurance companies, medical practices that continue to shuffle mountains of paper, no consistent process to record and retrieve data, and a total lack of cost control or awareness of competitive costs.

Tom received a letter from our local health care services provider, along with a complimentary pill splitter. They were offering the opportunity to reduce his prescription drug costs. We learned something new that day: The drug manufacturers make drugs of varying strengths. For example, Tom takes Lipitor and we believe it is available in at least three different strengths. What we didn't know is the cost is the same for any of the three strengths. One could argue that the people taking the low-dose version are *really* paying through the nose. We aren't going to get into the issues with the drug companies; Congress is dealing with that, with the passage of the 2009 health care bill.

Essentially, our health services organization, Affinity Health System, was offering Tom a savings if he agreed to take the higher-dose tablets and cut them in half each day. The problem was, they expected him to do all the work and yet they wanted to keep 81 percent of the savings. As he read the letter and thought about what Affinity was proposing, he was pretty insulted. The following letter provides the background.

Oct. 31, 2003

Mr. Chuck R.
Director of Pharmaceutical Benefits
Network Health Plan
1570 Midway Place
Menasha, WI 54952

Dear Mr. R.:

I want to provide you with my thoughts regarding your Oct. 14 memo on the cost reduction of certain prescription drugs that are "flat priced."

It is admirable that you are seeking ways to reduce health care costs. It is no secret the pharmaceutical companies are overcharging U.S. citizens and their health care plans. A recent example is Eli Lilly's (and others') position on limiting the purchases Canadian distributors can make, in an effort to limit diverting back to the United States. Moreover, I find it interesting how many dinners are hosted by the pharmaceutical companies for doctors at expensive local restaurants.

As previously stated, it is admirable to identify ways of reducing the cost of certain flat-priced drugs by up to 50 percent. Your proposal is to ask your customers to take the time to cut 30 pills in half each month. For that, you are willing to share $7.50, or 19 percent of the total $39.75 in monthly savings (your example). You, on the other hand, absorb no additional expense and keep 81 percent of the savings. This is an insult to our intelligence. Please let me know if I'm misunderstanding your proposal.

My proposal to you is, I will cut 30 pills in half each month and share $7.50 with you. Are you willing to accept this? You do absolutely nothing and reduce your cost by 10 percent. If your answer to this proposal is no, then I think it is clear you are not sincere about working together to reduce health care costs in a fair and equitable manner.

Please let me know if this offer is acceptable to you.

Regards,
Tom Wilson

Mr. R. responded in a timely manner, saying the program was strictly voluntary. Further, the organization wasn't able to split the savings, saying "The reason is quite simply that our vendor is unable to calculate the difference in cost between a prescription with split tablets and the cost of a prescription of the smaller strength that isn't split." This isn't clear, but we understood it. Its systems didn't support it and it didn't have a plan in place to change it anytime soon. Out of principle, Tom continues to take his regular dose. We just can't reward bad behavior.

Easy-Fill Prescription

June 7, 1999

President (name omitted)
LaSalle Clinic
Neenah, WI 54957

Personal & Confidential

The purpose of this memo is to make you aware of a situation that resulted in poor customer service and unnecessary cost.

Background

In preparation for a cruise in February 1999, I needed a prescription refilled, which was written by Dr. Johnson. The prescription was for Chlord/Clidi, and I had one refill remaining before April 1, 1999. ShopKo would not fill it for me because your Dr. B. had retired. I called LaSalle to have someone phone in a "new" prescription and was told this wouldn't be possible. In order to obtain a new prescription, I would have to make an appointment with a new gastroenterologist and have him or her write me a new prescription.

I explained I needed the prescription refilled because I was going on a cruise the following week. "Sorry, nothing I can do" was the response. I then called the gastroenterology department and explained that I simply needed the prescription rewritten. Again not possible, and further, since Dr. B. had retired, I was considered a new patient and the earliest anyone could see me would be May 19, three months later. To make sure the receptionist understood what I needed, I repeated that I simply needed my current prescription updated. "Sorry, nothing I can do" was the response.

I kept the appointment for May 19 in order to have the prescription rewritten. After totally unacceptable service, to add insult to injury, La Salle billed me $60 for an office visit when all I needed was the prescription rewritten.

As I am sure you can appreciate, this is not the level of service your mission statement aspires to. I would like you to explain what should have happened in this case and remove the $60 charge from our account.

Regards,
Tom Wilson

On July 12, the president responded, "Upon contacting our LaSalle Clinic location, it seems likely they attempted to transfer your care to a new gastroenterologist. However, it may not have been necessary to schedule a visit at that time, but to schedule a future visit and simply have had the prescription refilled one time prior to scheduling that appointment." He removed the $60 from our account and asked Tom to contact him with further questions.

Lessons learned: Your health care system needs to be constantly challenged, especially if you are entrepreneurs like us and pay for most of your medical expenses out of pocket. We've discovered that most employees of health care organizations have no idea what a procedure costs. We always ask and no one ever knows. We've had health care providers tell us not to worry about it because insurance will pick it up, or tell us we have to check with billing.

Ask what each procedure costs and how it compares to local competition. As consumers, we need to change this mind-set. Also, demand that your provider posts prices on its Web site for common procedures. It is no different from any other organization. Write to the president or CEO of the health care organization you rely on. Make the organization accountable.

"Well, we actually did produce defective glass when your house was built. They should have notified you."

Chapter 14
Home Repair

FOLLOWING are two home repair examples, one involving hail damage to our vehicle, and the other, defective vinyl siding.

Hail Damage

Here is one we couldn't resolve to our satisfaction, although our insurance company defended its position with more facts than we had. We learned a thing or two about insurance companies.

We've had State Farm since college graduation for automobile, homeowners and liability insurance. It's a great company. Ask Warren Buffet; he's been trying to compete against it with Geico and knows State Farm is a tough competitor. If you're careful or lucky, and don't have many claims, State Farm's rates can't be beat. We know because we've checked from time to time. That is something you should do with insurance every three to five years, just to make sure you're still getting your money's worth. It isn't just about price though, and this example explains why.

On the flip side, State Farm works every angle to avoid paying big claims; just ask Sen. Trent Lott (R-Miss.). Like thousands of other homeowners, Lott lost his home when Hurricane Katrina roared ashore. He has not been able to get State Farm to pay for replacing his house.

So, like thousands of his constituents, Lott has sued his insurer, State Farm, which has stonewalled Lott and other South Mississippians who lost their homes, on the grounds that their homeowners policies do not cover flood damage, even though the damage was caused by wind.

"Today I have joined in a lawsuit against my longtime insurance company because it will not honor my policy, or those of thousands of other South Mississippians, for coverage against wind damage due to Hurricane Katrina," the former Senate majority leader said in a statement.

The suit alleges State Farm wouldn't cover Lott's total loss because it was caused by a storm surge from the Gulf, rather than by wind. It argues the policy is supposed to cover losses from storm systems, and damage from storms typically includes not only wind, but also storm surges. In the end, State Farm decided it simply wouldn't provide coverage in Mississippi.

More on our issue of hail damage and State Farm. In a basic sense, insurance is a simple business: Pay out less money than you take in, and invest the difference wisely. It's the in-between part that's the challenge. That's where those funny people come in who determine risk using highly complex algorithms and statistical modeling. The lower-risk they think you are, the lower your cost, generally. For some reason, if you go through bankruptcy, they will increase your homeowners insurance costs. I suppose there is some logic to that.

On March 29, 1998, a big storm hit and it rained golf-ball-size hail, bigger hail than we'd even seen in our lives. Tom was upstairs and could see it bouncing off a lower part of our roof. There was so much hail; it was truly a once-in-a-lifetime experience. As our son joined us in watching it bounce off the shingles of our eight-year-old home, we remembered our new Chevy Tahoe was outside in the driveway. Sure enough, when it was over, our Tahoe had been decorated with hundreds of dimples.

Tom, along with everyone else in the area, called our insurance company. He was impressed with State Farm. He was immediately able to reach the company, and it set up an appointment for an estimate the following week.

We didn't realize insurance companies use "SWAT teams" in disaster areas. For example, during Katrina, 4,000 claims adjusters were brought in. These teams have all the equipment they need, such as tents, computers, printers and, yes, checks. They set up huge temporary quarters and rely on ready-to-eat meals if necessary. Tom drove our car under a tent, and a team was all over our vehicle right away. In five to 10 minutes, someone handed him a repair estimate and a check. That's it. Done. Very impressive.

We hadn't thought as much about the hail's effect on our roof; it just wasn't something we had experience with. However, it wasn't long after the hail storm that many of the houses had trucks in front, replacing the shingles. We realized that if insurance companies are replacing roofs, ours may have been damaged too.

Tom phoned our agent and arranged an inspection. In State Farm's usual efficient and speedy manner, the inspection was completed on June 4 and a check left for the repairs. Much to our surprise, the check only covered "dings" to some sheet-metal covers and other depreciation, for a total of $1,339.71. Meanwhile, throughout our neighborhood, the sound of nail guns continued as shingles were being replaced.

Tom contacted a reputable local roofing company and obtained an estimate on a new roof. The cost was $9,060, $7,720.29 more than the check State Farm gave us. We naturally felt like we had come up short. We thought, "Hey, we've been with State Farm forever, we insure everything we have with it, and now, in our time of need, this is what we get?" Tom contacted our agent's claims adjuster with the following fax:

Jim:

This responds to the roofing estimate you provided me on June 4, 1998, in the amount of $1,339.71. I have subsequently had the damage estimated by Wendell D. at American Roofing, totaling $9,060. Attached is a copy of his estimate. Would you please look this over, and talk with him if necessary, and let me know why there would be such a large discrepancy?

I have also arranged for a third estimate, since these differ so greatly.

Tom Wilson

On Aug. 20, 1998, State Farm responded by hiring an engineering firm out of Dallas, Haag Associates, to conduct a thorough inspection, analysis and report on our roof. We were presented with a 12-page bound report, including pictures of all areas of the roof. The conclusion from the independent contractor indicated the roof shingles were not damaged by the hail, but there was evidence on the thinner, more malleable aluminum material, such as vent flanges, vent caps and gutters. Further, State Farm said its original estimate included replacement of these damaged items; therefore, no revisions to the estimate were required at that time.

State Farm keeps its costs down by having the resources in place to provide prompt, efficient service. The resources are also in place to ensure it doesn't pay out more than is required. Other, smaller insurance companies, without such resources, told our neighbors to have their roofs replaced and to submit the bills. Those companies simply didn't have the resources to manage the number of claims they had. In all likelihood, the insurance companies paid for unnecessary roof repairs. More than a decade later, our roof was still fine.

We didn't realize until this hail storm that, similar to ambulance chasers, there are hail chasers. These people descend on areas that have had significant hail damage. They distribute flyers door to door, selling new roofs. Some of the help they offer, in our opinion, was suspect. By our way

"The goal as a company is to have customer service that is
not just the best, but legendary."

of thinking, you're going to have a roof for a long time — do you really want to do business with an outfit whose office is an F150?

As of Jan. 31, 1999, we had not cashed the check that State Farm had given us the previous March. We were holding onto it until the last possible day, in case something happened to our roof. We believe that once you cash such a check, you're saying you agree with the assessment. Insurance companies may tell you that's not the case, but you may be in a better bargaining position if you haven't cashed the check. Obviously, you wouldn't want to hold on to the check past its expiration date, when your bank will no longer cash it.

On Jan. 21, 1999, State Farm followed up with us to determine the status of the check they had sent. During January 1999, we did notice a potential problem with our roof that occurred during a thaw. A light fixture in an upstairs bathroom half filled with water, most likely caused by a leak in the roof, we assumed. We had never seen that occur before and we had been in the house for nine years. We should also add it never happened again. We still can't explain it. When this occurred, we sent the following fax to our State Farm adjuster.

Jan. 31, 1999

Mr. James W.
State Farm
Claim 49-X401-937
Policy Number: XX-XXXXXXX

James:

This follows up on our claim. Since the damage occurred on March 29, 1998, we received two bids for repairs:

American Roofing: $9,060

Gary's Home Improvement: $11,236

State Farm: check # XXXX for $1,339.71; issued on 6/4/98, not cashed

We have not cashed the State Farm check because we wanted to see if any problems occur. The reason I am writing now is because during a recent thaw, a light fixture in an upstairs bathroom half filled with water, most likely caused by a leak in the roof. Moreover, a skylight in another bathroom is now leaking. I think it make sense for you to have someone come out to inspect this before further damage results.

Following the results of this inspection, we need to negotiate a fair settlement. The proposed State Farm payment of $1339.71 is a fraction of the average of the two bids I received from qualified estimators/installers.

You should know that many of the homes in our subdivision have had their roofs completely replaced.

Please give me a call this week, as I am leaving for vacation on Friday, Feb. 5.

State Farm responded on Feb. 2 via certified mail with a four-page, single-spaced letter, saying we were going to have to agree to disagree. The letter also presented how the arbitration process would work if we chose to pursue it. Essentially, State Farm and we would choose independent appraisers. The appraisers jointly choose a competent and impartial umpire. If the appraisers can't agree on an umpire, a judge is asked to select one. We would bear the cost of our appraiser and half the cost of the umpire.

At this point, we made the judgment that it wasn't worth pursuing. We figured it was possible our roof wasn't affected to the same degree as our neighbors' because we used higher-quality, 40-year shingles during construction. Moreover, our house faced a different direction than most and the pitch on our roof was much steeper than the other homes. The pitch could have affected the intensity of the impact of the hail, we were told.

In summary, would we have liked to have a new roof? You bet. But State Farm did a good job responding to our requests in a timely fashion. By defending its position with facts, it avoided paying perhaps three times as much for a roof that, in its opinion, wasn't required. This helps keep the company's costs down and our premiums lower, at least in theory.

We highly recommend State Farm. We've dealt with the company in Illinois, New Jersey, Texas and Wisconsin, and it is consistently good at what it does. It also insures all aspects of The CareGiver Partnership.

On the flip side, Sen. Lott and many other homeowners are not only disenchanted by State Farm, they are angry, and as previously mentioned, had filed a lawsuit.

Siding Replacement

There is a 1987 movie called "Tin Men," starring Richard Dreyfuss and Danny DeVito, about the people who sell aluminum siding, which is now vinyl. It is a funny movie, especially to Tom, who used to be a "tin man." A good friend's family was in the business of selling and installing siding, windows and storm doors, and he learned the fine art of the business, with the selling line, "Well, you know, Mr. Smith, vinyl is final. You'll never have to repaint."

Being a part of any business, you learn a great deal about it. Tom knew vinyl siding. That's why he found it odd that a number of newer homes in our neighborhood were being re-sided due to premature fading. Out of curiosity one day in 1996, Tom lifted up a section of our siding and found there had been a great deal of fading. It was installed during construction only six years earlier and was of high quality, because we believe in "built to last." There was also a small section of siding that appeared to have melted and was warped.

Tom contacted the manufacturer and talked to someone about what he discovered. The manufacturer arranged to have a representative inspect it, who said it had faded more than one would expect. Tom mentioned he had been involved in the vinyl siding business and thought it odd the siding on so many newer homes had faded. The rep said it may be because of paper factories in the area spewing chemicals, and said paint companies had to reformulate their paints in this area of Northeast Wisconsin. Tom thought this was suspect and not supported with facts.

The next step was to follow up with the manufacturer's technical service specialist, who needed to see pictures of the siding to determine how much fading had occurred. By this point, we had been talking with our builder and building supply dealer for about two years about this. We were at the point of driving this to a conclusion and being done with it.

We contacted the siding manufacturer, who responded in a timely fashion, requesting pictures and other information. Following is the letter we mailed with the information requested. We've also included a lengthy list of correspondence to illustrate the effort it takes to successfully resolve an issue. All the people we dealt with at Variform, the siding manufacturer, were polite and, we believe, wanted to do a good job. We think in this case they weren't properly organized to efficiently resolve customer service issues. We're certain if we hadn't stayed on top of this or been as persistent, it may never have been resolved.

As a reminder, there were two issues we were dealing with: faded siding and, in two areas, melted siding.

June 24, 1998

Ms. Tedra P.
Technical Service Specialist
Variform, Inc.
303 W. Major
P.O. Box 559
Kearney, MO 64060

Dear Ms. P.:

Enclosed, per your request, are pictures of the front and rear of our home. There is little siding on the front of the home; almost all is on the sides and rear. As you can see from the close-up of a section on the rear of the home, the siding has severely faded.

We have been working with our contractor and building supply dealer for years to resolve this. As you know, it can sometimes be challenging to create a sense of urgency.

Following is the information you requested:

Date of installation: July 1990

Date of purchase: August 1990

We are the original owners.

Style: Timber Oak, Silver Ash, Lot 0123; other numbers on the carton are 118 and stamped is 01034.

Amount of product affected: uncertain as to total squares; however, all product on house is affected.

Sincerely yours,
Tom Wilson

Our first e-mail to the company was June 24, 1998. We ultimately had our siding replaced, but were waiting for a resolution on the second issue, melted siding.

Nov. 11, 1999

Subject: Issue with melted siding, WC9800878

I e-mailed this to Tim M., customer service rep, last week and did not hear back from him, so I am e-mailing it to your main site.

This summer, I had our Variform siding replaced due to premature fading. Late this summer, I noticed a section of the siding had "melted." In other words, it appears a blowtorch or something was near it. There is no heat source nearby or pipes behind the wall. It needs replacing.

Could you please arrange to have one of your reps come out and look this over? It needs to be redone. Please let me know when this will be arranged.

Sincerely,
Tom Wilson

Subject: Issue with siding, WC9800878
Date: 11/11/99
From: Tim M.
To: Tom Wilson

Tom:

I apologize for not getting back with you. I did request an inspection be done by one of our reps for your area, and have not heard back as of yet. So I wrote another request for an inspection time and date. As soon as I know when it might occur, I will give you a quick e-mail to make you aware of it. If you should have any questions, please give me a call.

Subject: Issue with siding, WC9800878

Date: 11/19/99
From: Tim M.
To: Tom Wilson
Copy: emersoe@variform.com

Tom:

I have spoken with our sales rep for your area. He explained to me today that he had been in contact with Lynn about the claim. He should be getting back in contact with you for further action needed. <u>If he does not within the next two weeks, please contact me</u>. Thank you for your patience.

Notice the underlined sentence above. What we're being told is that if the sales rep drops the ball, we need to let them know. Why should we have to monitor their potential ineptness? What Tim should have said is, "I will make sure you are contacted by following up with our sales representative."

Following is a continuing string of correspondence.

Subject: Follow-Up
Date: Before 1/31/2000
From: Tom Wilson
To: Tim M.

Tim:

I did not receive a reply from you regarding our e-mail sent 10 days ago or so. To refresh your memory, you had a representative stop by our house to look over the siding, which warped fewer than three months after installation. What are the next steps?

I had sent Tim an e-mail about 10 days earlier and received no reply. In November, we requested a service rep look at the problem. Sometime during December 1999, a rep stopped by and told Lynn someone would be getting back to us. We did not hear anything, so Tom e-mailed Tim once, and now twice.

Subject: Follow-Up
Date: 1/31/2000
From: Tim M.
To: Tom Wilson

Dear Tom:

I am trying to locate the information and photos taken during the inspection. I have left a voice mail with the technical services manager who inspected your home and will *hopefully (another bad word)* hear from him tomorrow. I will keep you posted on the progression of locating the information on your claim.

Please let me know if you have any additional questions. Thank you for your patience.

On Feb. 1, Lynn received a phone call from the technical services rep, who apologized for misplacing the file and not following up. He said he did a "pen test" on a window and thought it might be bad. Tom did a coin test on the window and found it to be OK.

Unfortunately, during the inspection, the TSR did not bring a ladder, or ask for one, and therefore was not able to inspect the warped siding up close. He also mentioned to Lynn that there was a vent in the vicinity, which Lynn explained was a bathroom vent. He also said maybe the heat off the shingles was causing the melting. He told Lynn that they would have it repaired "this time." Finally, he said they would be following up with a letter.

Subject: Follow-Up
Date: 2/1/00
From: Tim M.
To: Tom Wilson

Dear Tom:

I just spoke with our TSM who inspected your home, and he said he has still has the photos and will be sending them to me this week. I am sorry for the delay, but I will process your claim as soon as I get the information and photos from the TSM.

If you have any questions, please let me know. Thank you.

Date: 2/22/00
From: Tom Wilson
To: Tim M.

Tim:

I last e-mailed the information below on Feb. 1, 2000. I have yet to hear anything back. Will you please take personal responsibility to follow up on this, or give me a name and number of someone else? This has been going on way too long.

Date: 2/23/00, 2:22:03
From: Tim M.
To: Tom Wilson
C: farrimj@variform.com

Dear Tom:

Below I have attached a document of the status of your claim. I am also making sure that a hard copy of the letter is mailed to your home address. If you have any further questions, please contact me. Thank you for your patience.

Subject: WC00-115
From: Tom Wilson
To: Tim M.

Tim:

Thank you for your reply. I tested the window and it seemed to test OK. I will have it tested again.

This was one of two problems. We have the same issue occurring between the first and second floor, which Ed was to inspect but didn't. Where do we stand on this section?

Following is a letter from Jason F., technical service representative with Variform, who was copied on the previous letter sent to Tim.

Dear Mr. Wilson:

This letter is in regards to the claim submitted for panel distortion on your Variform D/4 Timber Oak Weathered Cedar vinyl siding panels.

As you know, your home was inspected on or about the 31 of January by our technical services manager. After reviewing the inspection report and photos submitted, we have reached the following conclusions.

The distortion of the panels on the lower part of your home appears to be caused by sunlight reflecting off the adjacent windows. Our TSM tested the exterior of your windows for a condition known as collapsed glass. This can occur in double-pane gas-filled windows and can cause the type of damage present on your home. He discovered a significant amount of collapse in the exterior pane, and submitted photos showing the reflections of a pen held to the outside. The reflections from the two panes are significantly closer in the center of the window than on the edges. This may be indicative of collapsed glass.

It is known that collapsed glass has previously caused heat distortion to vinyl siding and will continue to do so until the problem is corrected. Below is a written excerpt directly from a window manufacturer:

Double-pane gas-filled windows: This applies only if window casts reflection on vinyl panels.

Collapsed glass effect on siding panels: has a concave appearance on outside and concentrates the sun's rays (it acts like a magnifying glass) and reflects on the siding in a concentrated form, causing the heat distortion.

The problems will likely reoccur in replacement siding until the actual problem has been identified and corrected. Unfortunately, we are unable to offer any other solution at this time. However, we have developed an internal policy for consistency and fairness in handling this type of claim. We are offering a one-time replacement of the affected material and an allowance for labor.

We are issuing credit for four squares of siding and a labor allowance of $90/square to Builder's Supply in Appleton. Allow approximately 15 to 20 working days from the date of this letter for the credit to reach the dealer. Then you will need to contact the dealer and provide any information it needs to process the credit for material and labor.

If you have any further questions, please contact our office.

Sincerely,
Jason F.

This is a nice letter from Jason, but it took a great deal of persistence on our part to get to this point. If you read the last paragraph of his letter, the onus is on us to contact the building supply company and to work out the details between it and the installer. As it turned out, the labor allowance the company provided for installation was completely unacceptable. Tom checked a number of prices in our area and wasn't able to find anyone who was willing to do the work for what the manufacturer provided. As a result, we had to go back to Variform and plead our case until the company ultimately sent us a check for $440.

Although Variform made good on its warranty, it required a great deal of perseverance on our part over several years. A process that started in 1996 wasn't concluded with the final check until Jan. 22, 1999.

Lessons learned: What should have happened is the company should have had people and a process in place to quickly resolve warranty issues. As soon as it was determined the product was defective, it should have coordinated the installation between itself, the building supply company and the installer. It shouldn't force its customers to be the general contractor and have to manage the process of receiving and disbursing the funds. We had pay the building supply company, then get reimbursed so we could then pay the installers.

Tom used spreadsheets to keep track of where the money was coming from and who it was going to — a process that should have been entirely managed by the company in order to provide excellent customer service. After all, they are the ones who manufactured the defective product. We were just attempting to get our money's worth.

Andersen Window Replacement

Unfortunately for Andersen, our melted siding issue that precedes this example led to an expensive warranty repair for the window manufacturer. When we discovered a portion of our siding appeared to have melted, the reason given was defective windows.

We contacted our building supply dealer and it gave us the name of an Andersen representative. Tom explained our situation, and he agreed to come to our house and test our windows. By way of technical background, thermal windows have gas that is trapped between two panes of glass to improve their ability to insulate; that description may not be entirely accurate, but it will suffice for the purpose of this example.

The two planes of glass in the window are designed to be perpendicular to one another. In a defective window, if the gas escapes, the two panes of glass can become concave. The window loses much of its insulating properties and, because the panes of glass become concave, they can act as a magnifying glass, reflecting the sun.

After testing our windows, the Andersen representative found most were defective. He also admitted that at the time our windows were manufactured, Andersen had received a lot of defective glass. Our house was constructed in 1990, 10 years before this occurred. When we heard this, we wondered why no attempt was made to locate where the defective windows were installed. We also wondered how much extra we had paid in energy bills over the past decade because of defective windows.

Andersen agreed to replace all the defective windows, a total of 53 windows with a retail value of more than $20,000. The type of windows in our house require staining. Andersen did not agree to cover this cost, which amounted to $777.38. After Tom kept pushing, the company agreed to reimburse us for this expense, although it took additional follow-up on our part to ultimately get the check.

Following is correspondence with its local representative.

June 2, 2000

Mr. Michael P.
Manufacturer's Representative
Andersen Windows, Inc.
3134 Cutler Court
Oshkosh, WI 54904

Dear Mike:

As requested, enclosed is an invoice for $777.38 for the cost to have approximately 53 defective replacement windows stained.

"There are no traffic jams along the extra mile."

Background

In 1990, we had a new home constructed and instructed our builder to spec Andersen windows. We willingly paid a premium over other brands, because we wanted quality windows that would provide long-lasting energy efficiency.

During 1994/1995 we noticed some of our vinyl siding had a melted appearance. We had that section re-sided. Soon after, it happened again. We again had it re-sided, and again it melted right away. The siding manufacturer, Variform, sent a technical representative to inspect the problem. After testing several windows, he said the window closest to the melting was defective, causing the sunlight to reflect onto the siding. I have arranged to have the siding in this area replaced a third time.

Mike, we appreciate you and Andersen agreeing to reimburse us for the cost to have the replacement windows stained. As a result, we will continue to be Andersen customers in the future. We have built three houses already, all with Andersen windows.

In closing, a study conducted by Technical Assistance Research Programs, Inc., which was commissioned by the U.S. Department of Consumer Affairs, found 96 percent of consumers won't let you know they are dissatisfied; of these, up to 90 percent won't buy again from your company; you can win back up to 70 percent of customers by resolving the problem; and if you handle problems quickly and well, 95 percent will become loyal customers.

Thank you in advance for your quick handling of this issue. Please call me with any questions.

Regards,
Tom Wilson

We had to follow up with Mike regarding reimbursement for having the windows stained. Following is his e-mailed reply.

Subject: Warranty Reimbursement
Date: 8/3/00
From: Mike P.
To: Tom Wilson

Tom, I'm sorry I hadn't gotten back to you, but I haven't been able to find out anything yet. I did send in the proper forms back on June 5 to get you reimbursed for $777.38. The people at headquarters are supposed to get back to me on where it went from there, and I haven't heard anything yet. I will let you know as soon as I find out what's going on.

I will be on vacation until Monday the 7th.

Take care,
Mike

Obviously, we felt good about getting the new windows. However, we were only trying to get our money's worth. We specified Andersen Windows when we designed the house. They cost more but they had a reputation as a good window, and as we've said before, we like to buy quality.

Andersen ultimately made good, covering the cost of the new windows, the installation and the staining. It took a good deal of work on our part, many phone calls and e-mails. If we hadn't been persistent from start to finish, it's no telling what our energy bills would be today, with 53 defective windows during Wisconsin winters. We don't even want to think about the cost.

We still wonder why the company wasn't proactive in locating us to let us know there was a problem with the glass when the windows were manufactured. We're sure if we hadn't pursued this, nothing would have happened. We don't know Andersen's systems and capabilities, but here is a clear example of how systems could have helped improve customer service. If the company had a system to identify where shipments by lot were made, it could have identified the defective lots, located the ship-to addresses, such as to building supply companies, and asked for their resale records.

Lessons learned: In summary, we're glad we have new windows and appreciate Andersen's help. It did the right thing. We likely will build another house and it too will include Andersen windows.

The value of the new siding and windows, including the labor to install each, was well over $30,000. Without the pressure on the companies and continual follow-up, nothing would have happened. We certainly weren't delighted with either of the companies, because we only got what we deserved and it took a long time and a great deal of perseverance.

This is why it is so important for consumers to learn how to get their money's worth when things go wrong. This is also helpful to manufacturers, because they get a better understanding of where there are deficiencies in their customer service.

Bathroom Repair

This is a typical example of the building trade and why it continues to have such a tarnished reputation. In fact, the building trade has significantly more complaints to the Better Business Bureau than any other business

segment. We like builder/contractors; one of our closest friends from our Naperville, Illinois, high school is one.

In 1990, we contracted to build a house in Neenah. This was the third home we had had built in 12 years, so we were experienced in the process. We selected a high-quality builder with a good reputation in our area. He was certainly not low cost, but again, we believe in paying for quality.

When the home was completed and we closed, the cost was much higher than what was agreed upon. We requested details of the plumbing bills, masonry and cabinetry. Tom took a day off from work and tore through the mountain of papers, creating a number of spreadsheets. We ultimately negotiated a cost reduction exceeding $10,000. We found that cabinets installed in a neighbor's home were charged to us from a subcontractor. We were overcharged for the cost of our brick. We were charged double for sinks; we had molded marble sinks installed instead of the standard type and were charged for the upgrade, but not credited for the standard sinks that weren't installed. As busy as Tom was at work, the day he took off to analyze the costs turned out to be the most he'd ever made in a single day: $10,000+. Time well spent.

Our builder didn't conspire to overcharge his customers. We do believe there are a number of builders who just aren't good businesspeople and don't have the proper systems to account for costs. The joke with builders is they have accounts receivable in their right pockets and accounts payable in the left pockets.

After living in our home for 10 years, we discovered there had been a slow water leak that became evident. We had a plumber look at it and he determined the separate shower and tub units were incorrectly installed, resulting in a repair cost of $7,749.

We took detailed, close-up photographs and mailed them to our original builder, seeking partial reimbursement. On June 5, 2002, we made him aware of the situation. We followed up on Sept. 9 after the work had been completed, and then again after we settled with our insurance company. Our builder had been very receptive to reimbursing us for a portion of the cost, since the original installation was defective. The close-up pictures and testimonials from the other tradespeople were testimony of this fact.

After the work was completed, we responded to his request for a settlement proposal. We proposed we split the cost; the net of what our insurance company had already reimbursed us for. He seemed agreeable and said he would contact his insurance company first to determine what it they would cover. Following are two letters Tom sent him.

Sept. 9, 2002

Mr. Bob S.
Wood Builders, Inc.
1524 W. Spencer St.
Appleton, WI 54914

Dear Bob:

This is a follow-up to our June 5 letter regarding the reconstruction of our master bath. We have had all the work completed and the bills paid. The total cost was $7,749. I am submitting the expenses to our insurance company and we will negotiate what they are willing to cover. After I complete discussions with them, I'll get back to you on our settlement.

Regards,
Tom Wilson

After Sept. 9, 2002

Mr. Bob S.
Wood Builders, Inc.
1524 W. Spencer St.
Appleton, WI 54914

Dear Bob:

This is a follow-up to our Sept. 9 letter regarding the reconstruction of our master bath. As I mentioned, the total cost of the master bath repair was $7,749, of which I negotiated a payment from State Farm of $1,708.88 (gross). Subtracting a $250 deductible cost and faucets we upgraded, our out-of-pocket cost was $5,609. In your phone message, you asked what I was seeking. I propose we split this and you reimburse me $2,804.

To reinstate the issues, the solid surfaces for the shower walls (Lippert) were not properly joined with the shower base. Only a thin line of caulk provided a seal. Moreover, the shower base did not include a lip to form a seal. This can be confirmed with the owner of Turek's Plumbing and is clearly evident in the pictures I previously mailed you. This situation led to a hidden leak over a long period of time. Water seeped into the subfloor, requiring it to be rebuilt and new vinyl installed. A new shower enclosure was also required, because the rebuilt shower required slightly altered dimensions. This can be confirmed with Ed.

Within the shower, there was a solid surface ledge to place shampoos on, which was not installed properly. It didn't allow water to drain and, therefore, water pooled on the surface. This required rebuilding and was included as part of the shower rebuild.

One piece of solid surface attached to a wall had serious warping and required replacement.

The base for the whirlpool bathtub was not installed correctly. Again, this is clearly illustrated in the photos we mailed to you previously. The tub was removed, a base installed and the tub reinstalled.

We feel splitting the balance is fair and equitable because:

- Clearly there were issues with the original installation, corroborated by the photos.

- It is not reasonable that a bathroom should require this level of reconstruction within 12 years.

- Since the house is 12 years old, we have taken into account depreciation by covering half of the out-of-pocket expense.

Please contact us with any questions you may have. Any technical questions can be directed to:

Turek's Plumbing

Floors by Roberts

Service Glass

State Farm Insurance

Insulation & Supply Co. (Lippert)

Best regards,
Tom Wilson

Months went by and Bob didn't get back to us. Tom phoned him again and was told he hadn't heard back from his insurance company yet, but would follow up. By his own admission, he still had the photos we sent him.

Once again, several months went by and he didn't get back to us, so Tom phoned again. This time he said he was going to follow up with his insurance company. Tom asked Bob directly if he had any intention of reimbursing us, and he said he wanted to see what his insurance company would cover. He never got back to us after that, and we've since written it off.

Lessons learned: We tried to be reasonable and fair. We feel that Bob (not his real name) lied to us. He could have simply said he had no intention of accepting a portion of responsibility for substandard workmanship. We certainly wouldn't build with him again, nor would we recommend him to anyone else. This case was especially surprising to us, since we live in a smaller community and a reputation can quickly become damaged.

This next example relates to the bathroom repair project where we were charged for work not performed. You have to stay on top of your business, follow up immediately when you discover an issue, and be direct, factual and assertive in what you ask for. After all, you're just trying to get your money's worth.

June 21, 2002

Floors by Roberts

Enclosed is a check in the amount of $434.25. This amount is based on the original invoice minus the $75 charge to install vinyl at the face of the tub. We decided not to have this part of the work done.

Two entries on your invoice are incorrect:

- Prepare floor, cut bad subfloor — This was performed by our carpenter before the installers arrived; you didn't do this.

- Remove old material — This wasn't on the original invoice and I didn't ask for this to be done.

Sincerely,
Lynn Wilson

Lessons learned: This is another example where it was simpler to deduct the amount from the invoice. We never heard back from this company.

Water Heater Woes

Ask yourself, how long would you expect a new water heater to last? Some may say, it depends on the number of people in the household, the capacity of the heater and other factors. We're sure that's all true.

We've had four water heaters in the past 20 years. When we built our home in August 1990, there were five people living in the house. That's a good number of clothes to wash and baths and showers to take, especially when you have daughters. During March 2003, our water heater began leaking. We thought it should have lasted longer, but given that it supported five people for 13 years, that must have fallen within the bell-shaped curve of life expectancy. We had it replaced with the same brand. Our new water heater began leaking a year later, in March 2004. We had it replaced with the same brand and it was covered under warranty — that is, except the $118.71 in labor to install it.

The plumbing company we use is great. It did the plumbing when we had our house built, and we've used the company ever since. When we received the bill for the labor, we felt we shouldn't have to pay for that; it should be the manufacturer's responsibility. A water heater should last longer than a year, and we'd been loyal and stayed with the same brand for 14 years at that time.

We wrote the following letter to the president of the manufacturer, pleading our story and requesting a refund. This is another example of being rational and calm, using sound logic, appealing to a company's sense of rewarding its loyal customers, and providing a specific and reasonable request.

In this case, the company provided excellent customer service. We received a check for the service cost to install the new water heater.

April 14, 2004

Mr. Paul J.
President and COO
A.O. Smith
11270 W. Park Place
Milwaukee, WI 53224

Dear Mr. J.:

The purpose of this letter is to request a refund of $118.71 for labor to install a new A.O. Smith water heater, due to defects with previous A.O. Smith water heaters. I had e-mailed your company two times over the past month about this issue and never received a reply. Therefore, I am contacting you directly so you will personally resolve this quickly.

The original water heater was installed in new construction in August 1990. Due to premature failure, it was replaced on March 10, 2003, with a FCG-50. This product also failed prematurely and was replaced on March 2, 2004, with another A. O. Smith product, an FCV-50. Attached is the invoice from Jim's Plumbing, which has done all the installations.

I don't think a reasonable person would expect to be on a third water heater in 14 years. We've been loyal and remained with your brand. Therefore, I am requesting reimbursement for the labor to change out the defective product.

I would also suggest you look into your Web-based customer service. I never received a reply after making contact on two separate occasions.

Thank you in advance for taking care of this.

Regards,
Tom Wilson

He responded and they reimbursed us for the installation.

"How come when I charge something, it takes you a nanosecond before it's on my account, but it takes you more than four months to send me my rewards?"

Chapter 15

Rewards. Really? Credit Cards

EACH year the credit card industry mails 5 billion credit card offers. About 4,970,000 are not acted upon. They actually think they are doing a pretty good marketing job. We know this because Tom consulted with one of the largest banks in the world that owns a number of credit card brands.

It seems like every time you shop, the person at the checkout wants to sign you up for a credit card or credit offer; this includes Target, Best Buy, Marshall Field's and others. Why is that? It's simple economics: There is much money to be made in extending credit. Think about it. Unlike manufacturing automobiles, which requires massive factories, mountains of inventory and an enormous capital investment, the credit card industry is selling thin air. In fact, in today's digital, Internet-based economy, they're virtually providing nothing more than the connection of a string of zeros and ones to allow you to make a transaction. Even printed paper statements have gone by the wayside.

Tom has done a good deal of marketing consulting for credit cards companies, which are banks, as a partner with CenterBrain Partners (centerbraininc.com). Tom spent 30 years working at companies that actually manufactured products that benefited people's lives. As he got more involved with credit cards, besides considering the companies to be selling not much more than thin air, he also learned, after talking with hundreds of U.S. consumers about credit cards, that consumers view them as inherently evil. And that was before the financial crisis.

What then can the banks do to differentiate themselves? After gaining input from these consumers, it became clear that, all things being equal, service would be an important reason for people to choose one credit card over another. In fact, we learned that if you told people that all their customer service calls would be answered in the United States, that was motivating to them.

Our primary credit card is a Quicken Visa card issued by Citibank. We chose it because, at the time, it was the only card that allowed us to download our transactions into the Quicken software program. We had been using Quicken for about eight years and thought this card would simplify our finances.

Throughout our association with Citibank, we had an occasion or two where they were late crediting payments to our account and attempted to charge us penalties, interest and late fees. Through perseverance, we managed to have all these charges removed. We did discover that Citibank made customer service challenging, at least with us. We felt like they thought they were doing us a favor by removing the inappropriate charges.

In September 2004, we received a postcard in the mail from Citibank's credit card reward program, informing us we could redeem points for cash from our Quicken Visa Citibank rewards program. Let's stop right here for a moment — why does our credit card have three brand names? It's a Visa, it's issued by Citibank and it's branded Quicken, a brand owned by Intuit.

In credit card marketing parlance, there is a term called "affinity marketing." Some say it was invented by a company in Boston named Kessler Financial Services. The affinity with this card is the relationship between Citibank and Quicken. Citibank is licensing the brand name Quicken from Intuit. Therefore, Citibank is the licensee and Intuit, the licensor. However, as Ron Popeil always said on television, "But wait, there's more." Citibank also has a rewards program connected with this credit card, named Traveler Rewards. A person earns points by using the card, and these points can be used for travel, gift cards and, yes, even cash back.

"We are what we repeatedly do. Excellence, then, is not a single act, but a habit."

This takes us back to September 2004, when we received an offer to redeem points for cash. On Oct. 1, Tom dialed a toll-free number printed on the postcard. He told the customer care representative that he wanted to redeem 150,000 points for a credit of $1,500 off our credit card balance. Tom asked for, and was provided with, a transaction number. He wrote this number on the postcard, recorded the date he phoned, and waited for the $1,500 credit to appear on our statement.

After waiting two months, he phoned to inquire about the credit. He was told it could take up to two billing cycles for the credit to post to the account, but that it "should" be completed in a day or two.

From a customer service perspective, why does it take Citibank up to two billing cycles to post a credit, and yet if we use the card, the charge is debited against our account in about 48 hours? We think the answer is, it isn't willing to invest in the systems or resources necessary to allow this to happen. It wants its money fast, but wants to hold onto yours as long as possible. Banks and credit card companies definitely aren't looking out for you.

Tom waited a few more days and called again on Dec. 30 to inquire. The offices must have been closed because no one answered. On Jan. 3, he phoned again and was told that they were working on crediting our balance. Not satisfied with that answer, he asked to talk with a supervisor and was put on hold. When the person picked up again, she said our credit "should" be posted to our account within seven to 10 days. Tom requested the name and telephone number of the supervisor who would be responsible for following up on our issue. The representative would not provide a name or direct line, and said he'd have to call the toll-free number and ask for a supervisor.

On Jan. 5, Tom mailed letters to the CEOs of both Citibank and Intuit, explaining the situation and asking for their help. On Jan. 10, he phoned again and was told they couldn't help and would transfer his call to

Citibank. Confused, he asked who he had been talking with all along and was told "they" just handled the rewards.

The customer service rep gave Tom a "ticket number" and transferred him to someone at Citibank, who said he couldn't help and transferred him to yet another person, who then transferred him to a supervisor named Jennifer. Jennifer said she would pass along the question. When Tom asked for a specific person and direct phone line so he could follow up with a person, not a department, he was transferred to a Mrs. B.

He explained our situation to Mrs. B.and asked for her direct line. She said that even though she was a supervisor at Citibank, she did not have a direct line. In order for Tom to reach her, he'd have to navigate through the answering system, ask for a supervisor and leave a message. Mrs. B., from the Floor Redemption Center, suggested she could look into our issue and call us back.

A short time later, she phoned back with a supervisor, Lydia, on the line with her. Lydia, he learned, was from Atlanta. He later determined, by asking a number of questions, that she worked for a third-party vendor hired by Citibank to fulfill the cash-back reward requests, a company named ESC Loyalty, located in Roswell, Georgia. We later learned ESC, Enhancement Services Corp., was owned by Tsys Loyalty. Our Visa card was really a Visa card marketed by Citibank in New York, which had licensed the Quicken brand from Intuit in California, and had hired ESC Loyalty in Atlanta, who was owned by Tsys Loyalty, to manage its rewards program. With all these organizations involved, it isn't surprising that no one takes responsibility. Read on.

Lydia said our request was stuck in the Information Technology Department and all she could do was to forward it. She also suggested talking with someone in customer service. Tom told her he thought that's who he'd been talking to, before finally begging her to take the lead, follow though and solve our issue. Again he requested a name and direct line and was told that even at the director level, there were no direct phone numbers. He asked how people inside ESC Loyalty reached one another. Certainly there must be an online or hard copy directory. Lydia said one didn't exist. We know better and she should have been smart enough not to say something so silly.

Pressing further, Tom finally was able to get the name of Lydia's boss, Steve L., and his boss, Kenny B. He asked her to have Steve call him back, and for her to document our issue and send it to us via e-mail. She said she would do both.

We waited patiently for two days for Steve from ECS Loyalty to return our call. We also waited for Lydia to e-mail me the recap of our issue. Both promises were entirely ignored.

On Jan. 14, Tom called Lydia and couldn't reach her, so he decided to talk with her boss, Steve. Tom left a voice-mail message, asking him to return his call, which he did promptly. Steve listened to our issue and asked for a little time to check into it, only to phone later that afternoon and say our request was stuck in the IT Department, which, Tom told him, we already knew.

Steve asked that we give him until the following Tuesday, Jan. 18, to find out what was going on. Tom said he'd continue to be patient but asked Steve to think about what he was prepared to do for us, for forcing us to wait four months for a credit and having to invest at least three hours in 15+ phone calls. Steve responded by saying we would discuss that "if it came to that." Tom said as far as he was concerned, it had already "come to that," and asked him to think about what he was personally prepared to do to maintain us as loyal Citibank customers.

On Jan. 17, Lydia called to say she had been out but that her boss was looking into the issue. When Tom told her he had talked to Steve on Jan.

14, she sounded surprised. It was obvious the two hadn't communicated.

Steve had promised to look into the issue and call us with an update no later than Jan. 18. We waited patiently until Jan. 21, but he never phoned. When Tom called him, asking for a return call, he elected not to.

On Jan. 24, David from the "Office of the President" of Citibank called us in reference to a letter Tom sent his CEO on Jan. 5. In that letter, we summarized the issue and the steps we had already taken, and requested that a credit be made to our account by Jan. 12, which obviously didn't happen. David left a message saying he would look into the issue and would need "a few days" before getting back to us. We expected him to get back to us by Jan. 27, but he didn't follow up and Tom ultimately had to contact him twice on Jan. 28. The details of the conversation are as follows:

1/26/05 — Tom phoned Steve and left a message asking him to call back with a resolution. He elected to ignore the call.

1/26 —Teresa from Intuit's Office of the President called in response to our letter to her CEO. In summary, she said Intuit wasn't involved. She completely missed the point. Citibank and ESC Loyalty were wreaking havoc with Quicken's brand equity, since Intuit's name is on the credit card. We're sure there were many consumers who thought the issue was connected directly with Quicken. You have to wonder how companies decide which employees they place in the Office of the President.

1/28 — Tom phoned Steve in the morning and was told he was in a meeting. Since Steve refused to return our calls, Tom asked for his boss, Kenny, and was put into his voice mail. He left a message, summarizing our issue, and let Kenny know how disappointed he was with Steve and ESC Loyalty.

1/28 — At 1 p.m., Steve called Tom. We assumed Kenny had listened his voice mail, didn't wish to deal with us and pushed it back down to Steve — a clear sign of poor leadership. What Kenny should have done is return our call, then redirect Tom to Steve. Kenny must have been hiding under his desk.

Steve said our issue had been taken to the highest level and he would "try" to get back to us by the end of the day. He admitted he worked for ESC Loyalty, not Citibank, and it was experiencing a meltdown in its system as it related to the cash-back rewards program. Tom told him ESC Loyalty and Citibank should have been proactive and let the hundreds, or perhaps thousands, of customers know what the situation was.

At 5:32 p.m. Eastern Time, Steve sent the following e-mail (Tom had previously been told they didn't have e-mail):

Subject: Your Citbank Cash-Back Redemptions
Date: 1/28/05, 4:32 p.m.
From: Steve L.
To: Tom Wilson

Mr. Wilson:

I am pleased to report to you that arrangements are under way to issue you a check in the amount of $1,500, which represents the equivalent amount of the cash back that would have otherwise been applied to your account.

You should know that this is an extraordinary measure we are taking to find a way to quickly accommodate your request for resolution. Although it may have appeared to you that we were unconcerned about your issue, we are aggressively pursuing a resolution to this problem.

You can expect your check to arrive at your billing address by Federal Express no later than Friday, Feb. 4.

Thank you again for your membership.

There are four areas in Steve's e-mail that were poorly phrased, from the eyes of consumers who have been through so much simply to get their money's worth.

- First, he states the company is taking "extraordinary measures." From our perspective, without the incredible, obsessive brute persistence on our part, nothing would have happened. In our opinion, it was finally being forced to do something because we wouldn't go away. Moreover, we're sure ECS Loyalty didn't want us to do damage by further communicating with Citibank's CEO, Office of the President and others.

- The second word he should have avoided in his communication to us was the word "quickly." There was absolutely nothing quick in this entire process. Again, the company was being reactive vs. proactive.

- His third poor choice of words was "aggressively pursuing." We had already been waiting four months. We wouldn't characterize its actions as "aggressively pursuing."

- The last phrase that caught our eye: "Although it may have appeared to you that we were unconcerned about your issue ..." After waiting for months and with Steve electing to not return our calls, we would call that reality, not perception, that the company wasn't too concerned.

Tom responded with the following:

Jan. 28, 2005

Steve:

Thank you for getting back to me. I will accept the check and look for it no later than Feb. 4. The fact you are taking up to another week is beyond me. Where is the sense of urgency? FedEx could have delivered the check to me by Jan. 29.

Receiving the check only gets me back to square one — what I expected to receive at least two months ago in the first place. As you know, we've had to take extraordinary measures ourselves to get to this point. We had to wait more than four months for our credit, call ESC Loyalty and Citibank 15 to 20 times, and write to the Citibank CEO. We had to call David in Citibank's president's office. In total, we've invested well over four hours of our time. Had we not taken these extraordinary measures, I think we can both agree that nothing would have happened.

I had asked you several times what you were prepared to do to keep me as a Citibank customer after forcing us to invest the time and energy necessary to get us to this point. I would like you send me gift cards for Best Buy or Home Depot in the amount of $150, along with our check. This is a perfectly reasonable request, given the time we've had to invest.

The situation I have been through with ESC Loyalty provides a timely case study for a book we're writing about customer service. It adds a unique element of why it is critically important for organizations (like Intuit/ Quicken) to be religious about whom they license their names to (Citibank) and which marketing partner organizations they choose to associate with (Citibank with ESC Loyalty).

In the case of Intuit, who is licensing its Quicken brand name to Citibank, its image has been tarnished due to actions caused by its licensee,

Citibank's choice of a third-party vendor, ESC Loyalty. Citibank has damaged its image by choosing ESC Loyalty.

Steve, we all have choices. You will choose whether to honor our request. I will choose whether to maintain our relationship with Citibank.

Tom Wilson

To backtrack for a moment, David from the Office of the President had called Tom on Monday, Jan. 24, to say he would get back to him in a few days. We waited until Friday, Jan. 28, and still hadn't heard from him. Tom called him in the morning, then again in the afternoon, both times leaving a message to return our call. We left our home and cell phone numbers and e-mail address. When he called late Friday afternoon, he said he was waiting for our call. We hate to say it, but this is an example of an outright lie. We told him we still had his voice-mail message, in which he said in plain English he would call us in a few days.

David said he would be willing to "give us our points back" or we could wait until the following week to find out what the situation was. Tom told him that after four months, we would be willing to wait patiently for another couple of days.

On Jan. 29, we mailed a second letter to the CEO of Citibank. We also mailed a complaint to Eliot Spitzer, the New York State attorney general, explaining the situation.

On Jan. 31, Steve sent us the following e-mail:

Mr. Wilson:

Following up, this line is copied from an internal communication so that you can be sure the check is on its way to your billing address. I am forwarding your specific request for additional compensation direct to our Customer Care group. If endorsed by Citibank, it will arrive separately.

Check cut 1/31/05 for Thomas Wilson in the amount of $1,500.00, check # 43393, FedEx tracking # 791461888213.

Also on the afternoon of Jan. 31, David from the Office of the President, Citibank, called to say he had good news: He was working on having our account credited and should have resolution in a couple of days. After David finished talking, Tom told him he had been in contact directly with ESC Loyalty and it was sending a check for $1,500 via FedEx. David was completely unaware of this — another example of poor communication and total lack of regard for putting the customer first.

Tom had asked David what Citibank was prepared to do to keep us as loyal customers after we invested so much time and energy into resolving this. Tom suggested that $150 in gift cards would be appropriate, as it was 10 percent of the funds it owed us. David said he would look into it, and when asked if he had the authority to make this decision, he said he did. Tom asked him to take a leadership position and make a decision on the spot, but David said it would take him a couple of days to find out whose fault all this was. In an unemotional tone, Tom reminded him he had already taken a week and hadn't resolved anything yet. Further, Tom asked if we could both agree that the problem wasn't our fault. He agreed with this. Tom once again asked if he couldn't make this simple call and show some leadership; he was, after all, "in the President's Office." David said he would need to investigate it, but promised we would get the cards. To this, Tom said, "I'll hold you to that promise."

The fact that David either wouldn't or couldn't make a simple decision on a serious customer service issue is an indication that Citibank's customer service strategy needs a complete overhaul. If someone from the Office of the President can't make a decision, who can? After all, it wasn't like we were asking him to solve the subprime mortgage crisis at Citi.

On Feb. 1, we received a check for $1,500 from ESC Loyalty. On Feb. 3, we received $150 in gift cards for Home Depot. They were sent from ESC. The letter that accompanied the cards said the company "deeply apologized for the lengthy inconvenience surrounding the issue." The letter, which should have come from its director, Steve L., was signed by a customer care specialist.

David called a week later, on Feb. 10, to see if we had received our credit check and Home Depot rewards cards. On Feb. 14, we received a letter from David, apologizing for the unprofessional handling of our situation. Further, he stated the gift cards were being sent out and should arrive in seven to 10 days. We had already received them a week earlier. David's letter was dated Feb. 2. This, and the fact that he David didn't know the cards had already been delivered, made us question his ability to control a situation through follow-up. This is another example of lack of training and experience, lack of delegation to make customer service decisions and lack of attention to detail.

Lessons learned: From a consumer perspective, this case provides another textbook example of the perseverance and process required to bring a situation like this to a successful conclusion, so you can get your money's worth when things go wrong.

Be proactive — record dates, conversations, names and phone numbers. Be persistent and ask for specifics, such as when something will happen, who will be responsible, whom you should call. Get transaction numbers, confirmation numbers, tracking numbers, return merchandise authorization numbers — anything to identify your issue within the organization's database.

Try to deal with people, not departments. Make it personal, one on one. Maintain a professional and factual attitude, yet, at the same time, be demanding and assertive. The people you talk to don't have to like you, but they will respect you, because eventually they will realize you aren't a "normal consumer" — you aren't going away. They can't pigeonhole you like they can with most consumer issues. Many customer service departments work hard to make customers go away.

When you feel stonewalled, write to the CEO and, at the same time, keep up the pressure within the company's normal channels. Write to your state's attorney general and copy people in the company so they know you have. They don't want the government contacting them. Also consider contacting local television and radio stations and newspapers.

If you feel you have had to invest an abnormal level of energy and time to resolve your issue, ask the organization to do something over and above for you, but be very specific, as well as reasonable. Don't simply say, "I feel you should do something extra for me." In the preceding example, we felt that after all we'd been through, asking for $150 in gift cards was reasonable.

From a business perspective, let's look at what went wrong. We point to three key issues: people, process and procedure.

People

None of the people Tom was put in contact with at Intuit, Citibank and ESC Loyalty were empowered. This includes the individuals who worked in the Office of the President. Our "problem" was consistently pushed off onto another organization. Nobody took ownership.

Process

It was clear that neither Citibank nor ESC Loyalty had a process to deal with the issue. After 20 calls, they simply couldn't fix it. It was only after our letters to the CEO of Citibank that ESC Loyalty, fearful of its relationship with Citibank, finally decided to cut its losses and get us off their backs by sending a check. It was further evident there was a total lack of communication between Citibank and ESC Loyalty, and even within ECS Loyalty, where Lydia and Steve weren't communicating.

Procedure

There were no procedures in place to resolve issues with a sense of urgency or to manage them proactively. By their own admission, neither David nor Steve had any idea of the extent of the issue. Were they dealing with hundreds of customers or thousands? Both elected not to return our calls when they promised to do so. We would terminate both for being indecisive and for the poor quality of the decisions they did make. At their levels, they should know better.

The Home Depot gift cards that were sent from ECS Loyalty should have come from David at Citibank. After all, it was Citibank's credit card and we were Citibank's customers. We would think they would want to personally manage a damaged customer relationship firsthand and not delegate it. Further, ESC Loyalty, who mailed the gift cards, didn't copy David on the letter. We're not sure he had any way of knowing if the issue was finally resolved. Regardless, David elected to never follow up with us.

In the end both ESC Loyalty and Citibank each sent us checks for $1,500, plus the $150 in Home Depot gift cards. The $1,500 cash back turned into a total of $3,150. We don't espouse trying to get more than your money's worth, nor did we ask for it. In this case, we felt these two organizations deserved it. Moreover, we were certain they wouldn't have a process or procedure in place to manage a returned check. In the long run, we probably saved them money by simply cashing both checks.

If we were CEO of Citibank, we would put ESC Loyalty on probation and ensure they install a quality-control reporting system.

Finance Charge Reversal

In March 2004, Citibank was late in crediting a payment we had made on time. On March 17, we e-mailed the following:

The purpose of this e-mail is to request that you remove the finance charge of $109.88, which was debited to our account on March 16.

On March 4, we had an electronic payment sent by our bank, Bank One, in the amount of $3,317.88. It was mailed directly to your Payment Processing Center in South Hackensack and arrived on March 10. You did not post it to our account until March 12. Your delayed posting caused the payment to be credited after the closing date. As a result, you charged our account $109.88 in finance charges.

We would like this amount credited to our account and ask that you e-mail us back when this has occurred.

Thank you in advance for your help.

Citibank responded with the following:

We have submitted a request to waive the finance charges of $109.88. If the request is approved, you will see the credit on your next statement.

You will not be assessed finance charges on your purchase balance, if you did not transfer a balance from any other creditor and you paid your balance in full by the due date. Please allow seven to 10 days for your payment to reach us.

Finance charges for purchases, balance transfers and cash advances will begin to accrue from the date the transaction is added to your balance. They will continue to accrue until payment in full is credited to your account.

Thank you for using our Web site.

In response, we replied with the following e-mail on March 28:

I had requested a credit for a payment that you credited late and debited our account $109.88. I never heard back from you. Now I see you have also charged me a late fee of $35. I want this removed also.

In total, please credit our account $144.88 and e-mail me back by March 29 that this has occurred, please.

Citibank responded with the following:

Our records show the finance charge refund for $109.88 was submitted for approval on 03/17/2004. If approved, you will find the credit on your next statement, which will print on 04/15/2004.

We have credited your account today for the late fee charge for $35.

"When you serve the customer better, there's always a return on your investment."

Citibank ultimately credited our account and subtracted the charges, but not without perseverance on our part. We're certain if we hadn't followed up, we would not have received a credit. We wonder how many consumers are getting overcharged by banks and not following up? Who can track all this and who has the time?

After having consulted with one of the world's largest banks, who owns many credit card brands, we understand why many consumers describe them as being inherently evil. It is also the reason they are so heavily regulated by the government's Office of the Comptroller of the Currency, or OCC. On a regular basis, you read about the perhaps lawful but deceptive practices employed. One recent example is hiking interest rates if you obtain a new credit card. Beware.

"How do I know for sure your vehicle's not a lemon?"

Chapter 16

Turning a Lemon Into Lemonade

THIS **example illustrates** the hurdles involved in resolving a serious issue with a poorly manufactured vehicle. Even though we maintained and presented detailed records of the events leading up to arbitration, neither Chrysler Corp. nor the dealer would take decisive action to resolve the issue. In the end, we were forced to file for arbitration, and the arbitration board ruled in our favor. We decided to never again do business with this dealer, one of the largest in Wisconsin. It has now been more than 15 years and, not only have we never stepped foot inside any of Russ Darrow's showrooms in the state of Wisconsin, we believe we have dissuaded many people from purchasing vehicles from this business.

As our family grew and our mid-1980s model Olds Custom Cruiser station wagon grew tired, we began the search for a new troop-transport vehicle. Chrysler had created a new and popular segment, the minivan, specifically targeted for a growing family's needs.

At the time, there were few manufacturers who offered minivans. Chrysler clearly had the lead, and naturally, it was an option we considered. We did our usual survey of the makes and models and reviewed them in Consumer Reports. Keep in mind there was no Internet, so obtaining fact-based ratings was more challenging, and Consumer Reports was one of the bibles.

The Chrysler minivan, like many American-made vehicles at the time, were not rated well in Consumer Reports. Of particular note were significant issues with the automatic transmission. With this fact as background, we began shopping for a new vehicle.

One of the first questions we asked the dealer's salesperson was the validity of the transmission issues. He responded as a typical car salesperson, telling us they had in fact had some issues, but had "completely redesigned the transmission." In his words, "It was now the best in the business, world class." He did a good job selling us. They say the easiest people to sell to are salespeople. Maybe there is something to that — we've both worked in sales.

Using logic, we thought Chrysler wouldn't want to jeopardize the enormous success it was experiencing with the minivan by not creating a sense of urgency to turn this issue around. The salesman certainly seemed sold. The manufacturer's marketing teams sell the dealers on products, who in turn sell their sales teams, who sell the customers. We, as consumers, are at the bottom of the happy-talk food chain. It would have been nice to be able to inject truth serum into a Chrysler engineer responsible for the redesign and testing to find out how enthusiastic he or she was. Engineers tend to be more factual and not buy the sales and marketing hype. In our experience, research and engineering people sometimes cringe with the claims the marketing and advertising people come up with. That's why we think it's great for technical people to have good understanding of marketing and a backbone to stand up to them.

We're all for putting a product or service in its best light, but the fact is, consumers are smart. There is a saying: "Fool me once, shame on you. Fool me twice, shame on me." Not being upfront and honest is just plain bad business. If you tell us something that isn't true or is overly embellished in order to get us to buy your product, you should be ashamed. If we buy it again, it's our fault. The only vote consumers have is with their wallets.

Sometimes companies have a fairly strong lock on a product category. Microsoft has one with Windows and Office. If you want an operating system today, you may have to purchase Microsoft Windows. Chrysler had it at one time with the minivan. If you wanted a minivan back then, there was a good chance it was going to be a Chrysler product. The reason we mention this is to explain why we purchased a Chrysler minivan knowing that there *had been* significant issues. The fact is, there weren't many choices. We were also led to believe the transmission had not only been addressed, but the manufacturer had gone overboard to ensure it was now "world class."

We negotiated our best deal, including the trade-in of our beloved Olds Custom Cruiser, one of those old wagons with the rear-facing seat. It was fun to ride in the back seat, unless you were prone to car sickness, like our oldest daughter.

We took delivery of our new Chrysler minivan from Russ Darrow Group in Appleton. Everything went smoothly and we were proud new owners. We loved that vehicle. That is, until we were in Madison, 100 miles from home, for a football game and the transmission wouldn't shift out of second gear, which limited our top speed to about 45 miles per hour.

Since it was a Saturday and the Darrow Group had dealerships in many Wisconsin cities, we called for help, figuring it would tow our new minivan to its Madison shop, have a look at it and, if necessary, provide us with a loaner to get home safely.

Tom called and got through to the dealership. After explaining our predicament and pleading for assistance, he was told the shop was closing. He asked if they could at least tow it in and provide us with a loaner. Not possible, we were told. The dealership suggested we bring it in on Monday. Tom asked for Russ Darrow's number, a request that was denied. Frustrated and with no other options, we drove the minivan home at 45 miles per hour, with the flashers on the whole way.

The transmission issue was sporadic. Frequently, after parking and turning the car off, it would "fix" itself. That process however, didn't work in Madison. On the Monday morning following the Madison weekend, we drove it to the dealership. Of course, it worked fine then. The mechanics connected the transmission to diagnostic equipment and everything checked out. Our recollection is they changed a part or two.

We also began noticing that when the vehicle was in reverse, it would sometimes "clunk" (technical term!), then the shifting problem would present itself again. Several times we brought it back to the Russ Darrow dealership to have someone look at it. However, due to the sporadic nature of the problem, during inspection it would be fine.

So there we were, with a new vehicle that couldn't be trusted. We never knew if we'd able to get back home. We certainly weren't going to risk taking a vacation with it. And we couldn't simply shut it off and start it up again to correct it, because that only worked occasionally, such as when we took it to the dealership to diagnose the problem.

Frustrated, Tom wrote and phoned the business owner, who was in Milwaukee — 100 miles south of our home — and explained the problem. Tom requested a new or rebuilt transmission be installed, and the owner said he would "try" to have it fixed. Tom told him we'd had it in several times and the same problem existed.

After much dialogue, Tom made it clear how we felt about his service and the fact that, as the leader, he had not taken definitive action. He finally insulted us by saying, "How do we really know there is a problem with your transmission?" Tom asked why he thought we would make this up — what would be the point and who would waste the time?

Following this stalemate with no action on his part, one day the transmission acted up again, and we drove it to the dealership, this time leaving it in drive, with one of us behind the wheel while the other ran into the dealership, flagged down a salesperson, explained the problem and asked him to drive it. The salesperson experienced the issue firsthand and concurred there was a major issue with it, which we had him put in writing.

We reconnected with Russ Darrow and shared the evidence. He made arrangements to have the transmission worked on at his Appleton dealership. The dealership didn't replace the transmission, but did spend a great deal of warranty funds changing out a number of parts. At this point, it had already invested more in parts and labor than the cost of a new transmission, according to one of its mechanics.

We were now hopeful they had finally resolved the issue. Our recollection is that about six months has passed since we first took title of the vehicle. As time went by without an incident, we became more confident they had in fact fixed it. Unfortunately, it didn't last long and the same problem began occurring.

Once again, we pleaded with the business owner to replace the transmission, and once again were turned down. We brought it to the dealership a second time while it was experiencing the issue, to allow a mechanic to drive it. The mechanic himself said, "I don't know why we don't just replace the transmission."

At this point, we contacted Chrysler's national and regional teams in Detroit and Milwaukee. We faxed complete details, including purchase date, dates the transmission had malfunctioned, copies of warranty repairs, our letters to the owner and notes on telephone discussions with him. We wanted them to have all the facts in chronological order, so they could see firsthand what we'd been dealing with. Someone from the Detroit headquarters called while we were faxing this information and literally yelled at Tom, saying, "Quit faxing us so much; you're jamming up our fax machine." Sorry, but maybe you'll get an idea of what we've been dealing with.

While going around and around with the Chrysler people, we learned it's unlikely a manufacturer, like Chrysler, is going to supersede a dealership, especially a big one with multiple locations. The manufacturer isn't looking out for you; it's beholden to its dealers and wants to maintain good relationships with them. Our feeling at this point was neither Russ Darrow nor Chrysler was serious about customer service. Even after being presented with a mountain of documented facts over a six-month period, backed by evidence from a dealer's own mechanics, the Chrysler people were done talking with us.

What to do? We read the fine print in the back of our owner's manual to learn more about conflict resolution. Many of us are familiar with the term "lemon law." There is another remedy for major issues, and its called arbitration. Arbitration is defined as the hearing and determination of a dispute by an impartial referee agreed to by both parties. It's a simple, quick, inexpensive and smart process for the three parties involved: the consumer, the dealer and the manufacturer.

It begins with you, the consumer, completing required background information on your issue and attaching any other supporting details. It is obviously in your best interest to present a well-documented, unemotional, easy-to-read and understandable presentation of the facts. Being specific is important. By this, we mean dates; names of people you talked with; copies of documents, such as warranty repairs and inspections; and promised follow-up action.

After submitting a request, an arbitration board reviews it and decides if there is a case. The board is comprised of three parties: an average consumer like you or me, a trained consumer advocate and a qualified automobile mechanic. None of the individuals has any affiliation with the dealer or manufacturer. Theoretically, they are unbiased.

They reviewed our case and followed up with a letter stating next steps, which were to seek input from the Russ Darrow Group and Chrysler, review it and make a determination. The good thing about automobile arbitration is that it's binding on the companies, but not the consumer.

The legal term "binding arbitration" is a common practice. Companies like to use this because it can help reduce legal expenses and lengthy lawsuits. Unfortunately, it sometimes isn't as binding as it is intended to be, because companies use legal gymnastics and file appeals to arbitration outcomes.

We don't recall the exact amount of time it took to come to a determination, but it wasn't more than a month. We were contacted and told we would receive a replacement minivan.

But wait; there's more. We would imagine some consumers might think Chrysler was going to deliver a new minivan to our doorstep, free of charge. This is not the case. We understand the concept of depreciation. Since we had the fitful benefit of driving our Chrysler minivan for about six months, its value was less than that of a new one.

The next issue began when the people from Chrysler phoned. They were now very friendly. We remember our contact telling us that at Chrysler, customer service is extremely important. Our response to him was that they had a funny way of showing it. We reminded him we tried in vain to deal with this outside of arbitration but the company wouldn't cooperate.

He then presented us with an amount it was prepared to provide in order to replace the vehicle. Unfortunately, we've since discarded all documentation of this event, because it grew so large and became an uncomfortable reminder of the situation. We don't remember the specific amount, but it was quite insulting after all we'd been through with this minivan.

We do recall they must have created a new depreciation method outside of typical straight-line or double-declining balance methods, because we were stunned by the amount calculated for depreciation. We told our Chrysler contact we'd get back to him, and used the time to do homework and determine a range of valuations from normally accepted sources like Kelly Blue Book and others. Today, the Internet makes this easy to determine, but back then it was more challenging.

While we're on the subject, the Internet is one of the best things to happen to consumers. There are so many sites for reviewing product comparisons, features, ratings and pricing, as well as places to purchase. It has made buying fun and easy, and we believe it has saved consumers a great deal of money.

There is a concept in economics that explains why a person would pay more for a given good or service. It's known as "imperfect information." To illustrate, let say it's the 1950s, and you want to purchase a stereo system — hi-fi in those days. You'd probably go to your local appliance store, and you might even go to one in the next town over to compare. You rely on store owners to explain the features and make recommendations.

Today, you find a reputable Web site that explains the feature set in a given product category, such DVD players. The site outlines which features might be important to you and why. After selecting the features you're looking for, it provides a compatible list you can sort by rating, cost and more. If you see one you're interested in, you simply click on it and get a list of stores — retail and online — where you can buy it. You can sort this list by consumer feedback and ratings for the retailer, or by the prices they are willing to sell it for. You can even include your ZIP code and prices listed will include shipping. All of that in less 15 minutes, if you're good at it. Now, rather than just shopping several models in a few retailers, like you might have done in the 1950s, you've shopped hundreds of retailers throughout the United States or, in some cases, the world.

A friend of ours, who lives in Neenah, collects Russian war medals. How many people in Neenah are interested in buying and selling Russian war medals? Probably about one, maybe two. This friend says that since eBay created a global trading environment, the price of collecting these medals has dropped quite a bit. That's because there is less "imperfect information," and everyone who wants to sell Russian war medals is watching the other guys' quality and pricing, helping to drive down prices. Supply, at least known supply, is much more plentiful.

Back to the settlement with Chrysler. We phoned our Chrysler contact and made him a counteroffer, which included a significantly less depreciation amount on our minivan, supported with the research we had conducted. After some discussion, he had to check and get back to us, and we finally agreed on an amount. The way the process works is, you order a new vehicle, turn your old one in and pay the difference between the two. As we recall, the cash transaction is between you and the dealer, and ultimately, the dealer works out the details with the manufacturer.

The second part of our proposal to Chrysler was that we refused to purchase our new vehicle through the Darrow Group, because we didn't want to reward bad behavior. We suggested purchasing another Chrysler brand, a Dodge minivan, which at the time was very similar to the Chrysler. We had a local dealer in town that had an excellent reputation. Moreover, one of the investors in the dealership was a local person, who today is the largest car dealer in Wisconsin. Chrysler agreed to this.

We selected the new Dodge minivan and traded in the one with the transmission problem. We wondered about the poor soul who would ultimately own it. Interestingly, the new Dodge minivan had the exact same transmission problem soon after we took delivery. This time, however, our local dealer, Dodge Country in Appleton, replaced the transmission right away, leaving us to wonder why Russ Darrow hadn't provided this type of customer service. After installing the new transmission, the vehicle performed like a dream. We liked it and Dodge Country so much, we purchased another minivan from them and had it for many years.

Since the time we purchased the original vehicle from the Darrow Group, we've purchased 12 vehicles, at a combined cost of about $350,000, mostly fully loaded, high-margin vehicles. We never again considered walking into a Russ Darrow dealership.

As previously mentioned, we believe we've dissuaded quite a number of people over the years from considering the Darrow Group. We make the point again that consumer's vote with their wallets. Businesses like Darrow and Chrysler, in this example, need to place a higher priority on customer service. Leaving a bad taste in consumers' mouths can be very costly in terms of lost sales and negative word of mouth, especially in a smaller community. We are surprised that they either didn't understand this or didn't pay sufficient attention to the concept of a customer's lifetime value.

Lessons learned: The business owner and the manufacturer should have taken decisive action. There was no need for the issue to move to arbitration. The action that Dodge Country later took with the replacement minivan is evidence of this.

As consumers, it's unlikely we would have won the arbitration if we hadn't been diligent about keeping detailed records of the situation, taken the time to investigate our rights and prepared a well-written, fact-based letter "selling" our case to the board.

Our hard worked paid off. We saved thousands of dollars, got a new vehicle, and were able to do business with a dealership who earned our trust and confidence.

The Concept of Diminished Value

If you've ever purchased a used car, you're usually interested in its pedigree. In other words, you should ask, and the seller is obligated to tell you, if there is anything wrong with the vehicle that he or she is aware of.

You should also ask if the vehicle has ever been in an accident. If it has, you will likely be less interested in it or want to bargain on the price. This is the concept of "diminished value" that the insurance companies don't even want to discuss. It is covered in the finest of print on the thinnest of tissue paper they provide with your policy.

Each year, there are tens of thousands of automobile accidents. We had a nice car that was hit from behind, causing damage that exceeded 50 percent of its fair market value. Our insurance company, State Farm, did its usual perfect job processing the claim and getting the repairs started.

It dawned on us that when we sell the car someday, we would need to divulge that it had been in a serious accident. Even if not required by law, we feel it would be ethical to tell the buyer, even if that person didn't ask. All things being equal — car, model, price, color — a buyer will prefer to purchase one that hasn't been in an accident. The car that's been in an accident is worth less to a buyer, thus the concept of diminished value. It's based on sound logic and economic reality, yet insurance companies don't recognize it and essentially won't discuss it.

Our argument to our insurance company was that because diminished value wasn't specifically excluded in our comprehensive policy, that coverage is therefore implied. The most they admit to, which is stated in the policy, is, "In rare circumstances, the combination of repairs and other market factors might also affect the perceived market value of a particular vehicle."

In these cases, proof is required before payment is made. Under some conditions, diminished-value claims might be payable to a third party, under a policyholder's liability coverage. Again, proof of the alleged loss of market value would be required.

There are organizations that specialize in determining diminished value. One is Vehicle Information Services. It claims to be a unique organization that merges the experience and skills of vehicle brokers, repair specialists, attorneys, accountants and insurance professionals to provide sophisticated, accurate information. It alleges this interdisciplinary approach enables it to satisfy all of our vehicle information needs. It provides financial institutions, leasing companies, attorneys, government agencies, consumers, and the insurance industry with expert services and information regarding vehicles and their values.

The current debate centers on the auto insurance policy's collision coverage, and also on comprehensive coverage, which pays the policyholder for claims caused by such things as theft, glass breakage, flooding, hail and other weather-related events, and fire. Within the insurance industry, these are called first-party coverages.

Under some conditions, diminished-value claims may be paid under the property-damage liability coverage — called third-party coverage by insurers, which pays for damage to someone else's vehicle for which the insured person may be held responsible, if the damage can be proven.

There are different types of diminished value, including inherent diminished value and repair-related diminished value. Inherent diminished value is the automatic and unavoidable loss of market value when a vehicle has been involved in an accident. There are two types of repair-related diminished value: insurance related and shop related. Insurance-related diminished value can be defined as the loss of value incurred due to oversights and/or omissions by an insurance company on its appraisal. Another major factor that contributes to insurance-related diminished value is the mandated use of imitation replacement parts. Insurance-related diminished value can be minimized through properly completed insurance estimates and supplements. Shop-related diminished value is the amount which a vehicle's value is lessened due to improper or incomplete repairs, poor quality repairs, and/or unrepaired items that were compensated for by the insurance company.

"Although your customers won't love you if you
give bad service, your competitors will."

Those who support the concept of diminished value claim the car is "damaged goods"; there is a negative perception attached to the vehicle. They argue the car isn't worth what it was before the crash. They say it has automatically lost some of its value just by virtue of being involved in an accident. Currently, there are thousands of diminished-value lawsuits against Toyota as a result of the sudden acceleration issue. These have been consolidated into one class-action lawsuit.

If you were shopping for a used car and saw two identical vehicles on the lot, and the salesperson told you one had been in an accident and the other had not, which one would you choose?

Proponents further assert that if you are trading in your old car on a new one, and you disclose to the dealer that your car had been in an accident, the dealer will automatically reduce your car's trade-in value. You are legally required to disclose such information to a dealer or prospective buyer, so you may not be able to avoid the alleged loss of trade-in or sale value by keeping quiet about the crash.

Following is correspondence with State Farm on the matter regarding our car that had been rear-ended. Tom also had a long phone conversation with the insurance company's adjusters on the subject. When he uttered the words "diminished value," the conversation completely shut down. It wasn't even up for discussion.

We believe this needs to change, and insurance companies need to recognize it. Damaged goods are damaged goods. The insurance companies don't even allow repair facilities to use original equipment parts on repairs. You usually get "off" brands, which the insurance companies claim are comparable. You agree to that strategy when you take out a policy.

There is no question that if insurance companies had to pay for repairs and calculate diminished value, rates would go up across the board. However, the current situation today is such that if your vehicle is seriously damaged, you will suffer a loss on resale, no matter what your insurance company claims. These companies don't prefer logic when it works against them.

March 31, 2002

Mr. Seth B.
State Farm
Subject: Claim 49-3371-693

Dear Seth:

Attached is a receipt for a new battery that was required to complete the work on our Toyota Avalon. This was approved by your office. Since Bergstrom, the repair shop, had already closed out the job order, we paid for it. Please send a check for $114.07 to cover this expense.

I have a follow-up question regarding the diminished residual value of the vehicle. Due to the magitude of this accident and the repair costs involved — more than 50 percent of the fair market value — what is the process to reclaim this loss and what method does State Farm use to determine diminished value?

As you know, I will be required to disclose the level of damage and repairs when I sell the vehicle, and this will be like stamping "damaged goods" to the car's title.

Thanks in advance for your help.

Best regards,
Tom Wilson

I didn't get anywhere with the State Farm corporate people or our agent. At this point, the insurance companies don't want to discuss it.

"We know better than the Supreme Court what our donors want."

Chapter 17

Nonprofit

W E loved United Way and were strong proponents and financial supporters, giving even more than what it terms a "fair share" giver from the 1970s until 2001.

We knew our local chapter well, as Tom worked for Kimberly-Clark, who was by far the largest contributor to United Way in this area. He knew the United Way president, having led the campaign drive within Kimberly-Clark for a couple of years. Notwithstanding a limousine scandal that occurred in the 1990s, we continued to strongly and effortlessly be supportive of United Way.

That all came to an end when our local United Way board decided it had more wisdom than the U.S. Supreme Court and decided to ban the Boy Scouts from receiving contributions from United Way, beginning in 2002. This came after the U.S. Supreme Court decided the Boy Scout organization clearly had the right to set appropriate standards for the leadership of young men. Unfortunately, our local board chose to be politically correct and bend to a minority of special-interest groups.

Tom's colleagues, many of whom felt strongly for both sides, did not state their opinions one way or another, because they may be viewed as not embracing diversity. Tom clearly stated he felt the action taken by United Way was wrong. He suggested Kimberly-Clark should review its funding of United Way. Again, no one wanted to rock the boat. Tom told them he was contacting the president of the United Way Fox Cities, expressing his opinion and voting with our checkbook. The next day, he did just that and discontinued further contributions to the United Way. We haven't given the organization a penny since.

Our local newspaper received more mail on this issue than any other in recent history. Most of mail was against the United Way's decision. The paper printed an equal number of pros and cons, because it claimed it wanted to present a "balanced view." If it wanted to present a balanced view, it should have printed them proportionately.

We were really incensed when we discovered the United Way was accepting contributions on behalf of the Boy Scouts by passing them along after subtracting a "handling fee." You can't have it both ways; you can't accept cash in order to collect a handling fee, yet be morally against the Boy Scouts' so-called "exclusionary" policies. Again, many large companies accepted United Way's hypocritical strategy and continued to urge employees to give up their hard-earned money. With so many other needy organizations without a tarnished record like United Way's, Tom really lost confidence in management's decision-making abilities.

The point here is, as individual consumers, all we can do is vote with our checkbooks. We never reward bad behavior, whether it is with a business or, in this case, a charity.

Tom wrote a letter to the chairperson of our local United Way board, telling her how disappointed he was in her inability to take a leadership position and stand up to the politically correct elements within the board. Following is what he wrote.

Jan. 27, 2001

Ms. Linda K.
United Way Fox Cities
118 State St.
Appleton, WI 54911

Dear Ms. K.:

It's very unfortunate that the board and president have made the decision to eliminate funding to the Boy Scouts.

The Boy Scouts were one of your founding agencies. In its more than 90-year history, the Boy Scouts of America have served more than 100 million members and their families as a consistent platform for the values upon which America was built. I was a Cub Scout and a Boy Scout, and found it to be one of my most positive experiences.

As a values-based educational movement, the Boy Scouts of America asks its members to subscribe to the tenets of the Scout Oath and Scout Law. Instilling moral and religious values in young people benefits all of society. With the substantial number of fatherless households today, boys and young men need solid role models and leadership. For example, in the African-American community alone, 69 percent of babies are born out of wedlock. On June 28, 2000, the United States Supreme Court reaffirmed the Boy Scouts of America's standing as a private organization with the right to set its own membership and leadership standards. Unfortunately, by your president's own definition, the Supreme Court was not "enlightened."

The United Way does not implement a specific policy of nondiscrimination for individual charities, so as to avoid conflict with charities that serve only specific segments of the population, including women's shelters, programs for persons of a certain age group, or programs for persons of specific cultural communities. Unfortunately, it appears you and the board don't have the vigor to stand up to special-interest groups. Which agency will lose funding next? I would think the UWFC would want to generate the greatest level of contributions and leave "enlightenment" up to contributors. They, individually, can decide which agencies to contribute to.

You will have to categorize me as "unenlightened." Effective immediately, I am terminating our United Way contributions and redirecting these funds to other more enlightened charities. I have been a "fair share +" giver for more than 25 years.

Tom Wilson

As expected, many contributors did vote with their checkbooks, and United Way contributions decreased for the first time. A board made up of a handful of politically correct people caused many fine local organizations to suffer a decrease in funding. It then began "accepting" donations on behalf of the Boy Scouts, after deducting handling fees. This further reinforced our position that we had made the right decision. You can't be against the Boy Scouts, for diversity, inclusivity and the other happy talk, yet accept money for the Boy Scouts after deducting fees.

Ultimately, after several years, the United Way began accepting donations for the Boy Scouts, but have applied a few caveats surrounding those donations so they can save face.

Lessons learned: Unless you vote with your wallet, politically correct organizations — like this one that made bad choices and had a past history of abuse of funds, such as the limo scandal — will continue these practices. There are so many other organizations worthy of your contributions. To be clear, this decision only affected the United Way in the Wisconsin Fox Cities.

Now, go get your money's worth!

Chapter 18

Now, Go Get Your Money's Worth

NOW you are ready to begin getting your money's worth when interacting with any organization that seeks you as a customer, client, patient or donor. Medical service providers are very slowly grasping that they have "customers," not just patients. With almost a third of Americans without health insurance or with high-deductible policies, consumers are more and more shopping the market and questioning medical billing.

As we said, we belong to a large health system and it does not provide customers with posted prices for standardized procedures. We have been asking its CEO for several years to do so. Thus far, he has elected to ignore our pleas. As consumer advocates for 30 years, we will keep after him. Our next step may be to confront the issue in our local newspaper or through our public relations agency.

We urge you to take us up on our 100 percent one-year money-back guarantee for the purchase of this book. If you decide today to take control of your interactions with organizations, and follow the processes presented to get your money's worth, we guarantee you will save at least two times the cost of this book.

100 Percent One-Year Money-Back Guarantee

1. Purchase this book and save the receipt.

2. Read this book.

3. Anytime you feel you haven't received your money's worth, follow the steps outlined in this book.

4. Record the outcomes of your interactions with organizations, including any refunds, travel points, coupons or other compensation provided to you.

5. If, within one year of the purchase date of this book, your compensation does not equal at least two times the cost of this book, return it, along with your receipt, and you will receive a full refund. Simply send your book and dated receipt to Tom and Lynn Wilson, 333 N. Commercial St., Suite 350, Neenah, WI 54956. Tell us how you used the process to try and get your money's worth.

We would love to hear your success stories! We plan to include the best examples in the next edition of this book, so that we, as consumer advocates, can help others get their money's worth when things go wrong.

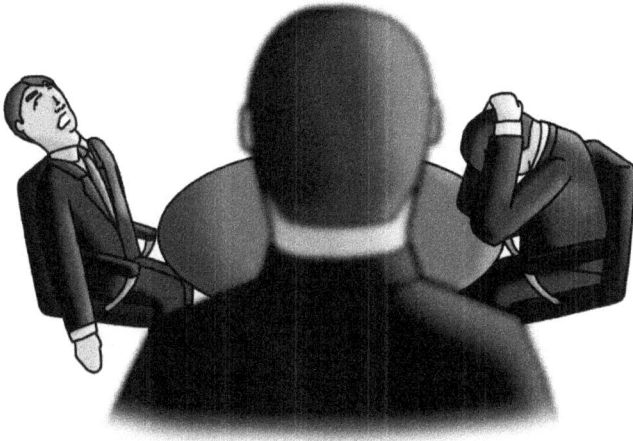

"At the end of the day, we need to ensure that we're all actionable with a strong bias for action. That's why today I'm empowering each of our employees to reach out and be laser-focused on being client-focused — in a proactive manner. We're re-engineering the entire process from end to end, and we'll come out of this transformative strategic redeployment with new synergies and as a world-class, transparent organization. I trust that's clear."

About the Authors

Lynn Wilson

In 2004, Lynn Wilson co-founded The CareGiver Partnership, along with her husband, Tom, as a natural extension of her many years of experience caring for loved ones and providing excellent customer service in the world of retail. Lynn grew up in Naperville, Illinois, and attended Northern Illinois University and the University of Illinois–Chicago, where she studied marketing and psychology.

Lynn was a stay-at-home mom when it wasn't popular. Now that her children are grown, she enjoys spending two days each week with her granddaughter, helps care for her mother long-distance, and is raising the next generation of her family, a poodle named Stella. In addition, Lynn prides herself on offering excellent Personalized Attention[SM] service to help her customers in any way she can.

Tom Wilson

Along with wife Lynn, Tom Wilson co-founded The CareGiver Partnership in 2004. Tom has 36 years of marketing and executive-level experience building consumer packaged goods businesses with Kimberly-Clark and Colgate-Palmolive. Tom was formerly president of Kimberly-Clark's global Feminine Care and Adult Care products business segments.

An entrepreneur at heart, Tom, along with Lynn, started their first company in their 20s, manufacturing underground coal-mining equipment. Later they sold the company to Alco-Standard Corporation. More than 30 years ago, Tom and Lynn began documenting customer service issues they encountered with various companies and organizations. They used these experiences to create The CareGiver Partnership, offering a whole new level of service to caregivers and their loved ones.

Index

www.ingramcontent.com/pod-product-compliance
Lightning Source LLC
Chambersburg PA
CBHW060345200326
41519CB00011BA/2040